StarGuard
Instructor Guide
THIRD EDITION

Jill E. White

Starfish Aquatics Institute

HUMAN
KINETICS

StarGuard Instructor Guide, Third Edition

ISBN-10: 0-7360-6076-6
ISBN-13: 978-0-7360-6076-9

Published by Human Kinetics, Inc., in cooperation with Starfish Aquatics Institute.

The Web addresses cited in this text were current as of November 2005, unless otherwise noted.

Acquisitions Editor: Patricia Sammann
Developmental Editor: Anne Cole
Assistant Editors: Mandy Maiden and Cory Weber
Copyeditor: Annette Pierce
Proofreader: Jim Burns
Permission Manager: Carly Breeding
Graphic Designer: Nancy Rasmus
Graphic Artist: Kim McFarland
Photo Manager: Dan Wendt
Cover Designer: Keith Blomberg
Photographer (cover): Dan Wendt
Photographer (interior): Dan Wendt
Art Manager: Kareema McLendon
Illustrators: Argosy and Kareema McLendon
Printer: United Graphics

Printed in the United States of America   10   9   8   7   6   5   4   3   2   1

Human Kinetics
Web site: www.HumanKinetics.com

United States: Human Kinetics
P.O. Box 5076
Champaign, IL 61825-5076
800-747-4457
e-mail: humank@hkusa.com

Canada: Human Kinetics
475 Devonshire Road Unit 100
Windsor, ON N8Y 2L5
800-465-7301 (in Canada only)
e-mail: orders@hkcanada.com

Europe: Human Kinetics
107 Bradford Road
Stanningley
Leeds LS28 6AT, United Kingdom
+44 (0) 113 255 5665
e-mail: hk@hkeurope.com

Australia: Human Kinetics
57A Price Avenue
Lower Mitcham, South Australia 5062
08 8277 1555
e-mail: liaw@hkaustralia.com

New Zealand: Human Kinetics
Division of Sports Distributors NZ Ltd.
P.O. Box 300 226 Albany
North Shore City
Auckland
0064 9 448 1207
e-mail: info@humankinetics.co.nz

Contents

Contents

Introduction

Welcome to StarGuard! The Starfish Aquatics Institute, which developed the StarGuard lifeguarding program, was founded in 2000 with a mission to reduce drowning and save lives by providing reputable and responsive aquatic safety training programs and services. It delivers these programs through a network of independent training centers operated by friendly, knowledgeable aquatic professionals. Starfish Aquatics' comprehensive strategy includes the development of training courses and innovative community-based projects, partnerships with like-minded organizations, and collaboration with other agencies.

Two organizations that have been involved with Starfish Aquatics in the StarGuard program are the American Safety and Health Institute and Human Kinetics:

- **The American Safety and Health Institute (ASHI)** is a not-for-profit association of professional educators providing nationally recognized emergency care training programs across the United States and in several foreign countries. Its mission is to continually improve safety and health education by promoting high standards for members, principles of sound research for curriculum development, and the professional development of safety and health instructors worldwide.

- **Human Kinetics** develops quality books and online courses for a range of professionals within the fields of physical activity and health. The online courses engage students in interactive activities that help them learn the subject matter in meaningful ways.

The materials for the StarGuard course include the emergency care text and instructor manual, StarGuard text and instructor guide, and accompanying online courses. You can teach the course in one of two ways. In one method, students study the texts, and you facilitate classroom and in-water activities. Or you can use a blended method that combines study of the student texts with two online courses. You then follow up with instructor-led water activities and scenario training. You also can provide supplemental training modules on waterparks, waterfronts, and wilderness aquatics for those who require additional training in these areas, either as part of the course or as separate modules.

StarGuard Curriculum

The StarGuard curriculum consists of five core components—prevention, surveillance, emergency care, aquatic rescue, and professionalism and personal safety—based on the Starfish aquatic risk management model. Prevention and surveillance, including victim-recognition skills, are integrated into 70 percent of the course. Aquatic rescue and emergency care (first aid) for a conscious person is integrated into 40 percent of the course, and rescue and emergency care for an unconscious person is integrated into 50 percent of the course. The course reinforces professionalism and personal safety throughout.

The StarGuard curriculum is superior to many other lifeguard training programs for these reasons:

- The curriculum is based on nationally recognized guidelines that integrate lifeguards into the EMS system by teaching them the same priorities of care and general approach to a patient that professional responders use. This promotes continuity of care as the layperson passes the ill or injured person to the professional.

- The curriculum follows nationally recognized protocols and guidelines that are safe and indicated for and helpful in minimizing the risk of injury and drowning.

- The focus of the curriculum is on following the most recent international guidelines for basic life support and teaching the primary skills of prevention and the ABCs, which stands for airway, breathing, and circulation.

Additional information is included based on its practicality.

Contents of the Instructor Guide

This manual is *StarGuard: Instructor Guide,* and it is intended for use by certified StarGuard instructors affiliated with an authorized Starfish Aquatics Institute training center (see chapter 5 for requirements for becoming a certified instructor). It can also be useful for aquatic directors, lifeguard supervisors, and instructors with other agencies who want to use an experiential approach to their in-house aquatic training programs.

In the past, lifeguard training has been modeled on standard classroom teaching methods in which an instructor conveys information to students through lectures or video. However, researchers in adult education have found that adults learn best when teaching methods include student participation. Therefore, StarGuard training is learner centered rather than teacher centered and actively involves learners.

This guide is organized into two parts. Part I contains information about the learning principles on which the StarGuard course is founded. Here you will find a wealth of information about how to train more effectively. As an instructor, you will be a facilitator rather than a lecturer. You will engage your students in active learning; they will work together to practice skills, and you will provide them with immediate feedback in a positive way. You will hold students to practical, measurable educational objectives and ask them to show that they can perform what they have learned in realistic situations.

Part II provides you with a step-by-step guide to facilitating a StarGuard course, beginning with a chapter on StarGuard administrative guidelines. The other chapters are organized into five block sessions that follow a logical and practical order. Each block session outline includes the following components:

- *Goals* presents the overall focus.

- *Skill objectives* lists what the student will be able to perform by the end of the block.
- *Average time* lists how long it should take to complete all the objectives. The time is divided into the percentage of time spent on wet (in-water) activities and dry (out-of-water) activities.
- *Overview* breaks down the session into subactivities, with a suggested time for each.
- *Text reference* indicates where to find information relevant to the activity in the *StarGuard: Best Practices for Lifeguards* and *Essentials in Basic Emergency Care*.
- *Materials* lists the equipment and supplies recommended for the activities.
- *Delivery* contains specific steps for each activity.

With the combination of a well-planned curriculum and a learner-centered teaching approach, the StarGuard course helps students gain the knowledge and skills they need to become excellent lifeguards. Students also are more likely to come out of this course with a respect for the importance of their work. We hope that you find teaching the StarGuard course to be rewarding as you prepare new lifeguards for this essential job.

PART I

Integrated Teaching and Experiential Learning

Principles of Adult Learning

Many, if not most, of your StarGuard students will be teenagers rather than legal adults. However, you are training these young people to bear an adult responsibility: preserving and saving lives. You must set the tone and treat your students as adult learners.

In this chapter we discuss how adults learn, first by briefly describing the types of learning that can occur and then by talking about how to present material in a way that improves adults' retention of learning. We also suggest ways to best communicate with the adults you teach.

Types of Learning

Learning can be classified into three types:

1. Knowledge. Developing students' knowledge of facts and information is also called cognitive learning. It includes, for example, the ability to state three methods of scanning as well as describing in detail the underlying reasons that it is important to scan. Cognitive learning is developed through activities such as reading or online learning.

2. Skills. The development of the physical skills needed to perform a task is called kinesthetic or motor skills learning. For example, a lifeguard must learn the skill of turning his or her head while moving the eyes in an established pattern before he or she can perform scanning.

3. Application of learning and attitude. Also called affective learning, this is the crucial component in getting a learner to perform, execute, or apply knowledge or skills. Consider the example of scanning: It is not enough for a lifeguard trainee to know about scanning or even for that person to be able to demonstrate the skill of turning the head and moving the eyes. Before that person can execute scanning, especially effectively for long periods of time, he or she must learn a sense of responsibility and obligation to apply this knowledge and skill. Further development of the desire to perform to the best of one's ability can, in the case of a lifeguard, mean the difference between life and death.

One of your most challenging tasks as a lifeguard instructor will be to instill in your students a sense of responsibility and a desire to perform at a high level. At the beginning of the course your students may not understand the importance of what they are doing or the consequences of not taking the responsibility seriously. If you find that a student does not respond to the challenge of being treated as an adult learner, this may indicate that she or he does not have the emotional capacity to accept the responsibility of becoming a lifeguard. As an instructor, you have the obligation to evaluate your students' attitude and maturity level and to deny course completion to anyone who does not exhibit behavior that indicates an understanding of the seriousness of lifeguarding.

Now that you know what types of learning you want to foster in your students, let's look at how you can best present information to your adult learners.

Adult Learning

The StarGuard curriculum is based on proven concepts and principles about how adults learn. The true test of learning is how well students can remember and apply what they have learned. The following list breaks down retention rates for the various ways adults gain information. Adults retain:

10 percent of what they read (student manuals)

20 percent of what they hear (instruction)

30 percent of what they see (illustrations, photos, demonstrations)

50 percent of what they both see and hear (video)

70 percent of what they say (discussion)

90 percent of what they do and say (integrated practice)

To maximize your students' retention of what they learn, reduce what you say to key points, and accompany that with skill demonstrations, discussion, and integrated practice. Adults want to be actively involved in learning, so you need to use interactive, experiential teaching methods. Experiential teaching methods are based on the theory that adults learn best in a hands-on setting followed by questioning and reflection of the learning experience. The StarGuard course is specifically designed to help you deliver a concise, effective course that will actively engage your students.

Adults learn best in an environment that is informal but organized so that they feel that their time is valued and that the experience is worth their time. Adults learn best if they are able to proceed at a reasonable pace that is not too slow or too fast. Immediate feedback is essential to the adult student, who needs to be continually informed of progress.

- Adults must have a clear understanding of what performance is expected by seeing someone demonstrate or model the skill.
- Adults want to know why they need to learn the skill by hearing the objectives. Motivation is increased when the content is relevant to students' immediate interests and concerns.
- Adults want to know how skills work, and they learn better if they are active participants rather than passive observers.

- Adults want to learn new concepts and principles; they enjoy situations that involve solving problems so that they can understand when to apply the knowledge and skill they have learned.
- Adults want to practice in scenario activities so that they can begin to reflexively apply the skills they have learned and gain confidence.
- Adults want to be respected and to learn in a supportive environment free from fear, threats, and punishment.

Understanding these principles of adult learning is crucial to your success as an instructor, along with the ability to effectively communicate with and relate to your students.

Application of Learning Principles for Effective Training

- Let the learner experience by doing.
- Make sure each activity has a purpose.
- Give positive, specific feedback.
- Guide and prompt; do not tell.
- Inform learners of objectives.
- Use realistic examples.
- Facilitate learning; don't just present information.
- Change the pace and flow.
- Remove the fear factor; expect high performance while being supportive.

Effective Communication

When you conduct a StarGuard course, you will communicate with your students both verbally and nonverbally. How well you speak influences your ability to present information verbally. Students will benefit from your strong verbal skills, which must include the ability to do the following:

- Speak clearly.
- Speak loudly.
- Speak at a comfortable pace.
- Speak in short, concise segments when giving directions; keep it simple.
- Humanize your communication with appropriate personal experience, but avoid lengthy "war stories."
- Ask open-ended questions to involve your students.
- Listen and facilitate as much as or more than you speak.

Your nonverbal communication skills will also influence your effectiveness as an instructor. Students will benefit from the professional attitude you project through your body language and manner as well as the climate and tone you create. The following will help you establish the appropriate learning atmosphere:

- Get started at a lively pace.
- Involve students immediately.
- Dress in a professional manner, appropriate for the activity.
- Maintain good eye contact.
- Stand relaxed, but with good posture.
- Stay focused. Do one thing at a time.
- Demonstrate skills with precise movements.
- Smile!
- Be active and enthusiastic, even if you have to fake it at times.

2

Instructor As Facilitator

Adults learn best when they feel physically and emotionally comfortable in a training situation and are led by an effective facilitator. When you are a facilitator, you guide students to learning. A facilitation approach is student centered, not teacher centered. Consider the following differences:

A facilitator views the training as belonging to the students. The facilitator's role is a "guide on the side."

A teacher or lecturer views the training as belonging to him or her. The teacher or lecturer's role is a "sage on the stage."

A facilitator seeks active participation.

A teacher or lecturer seeks passive listening and watching.

A facilitator asks questions and adjusts to meet needs.

A teacher or lecturer follows a prescribed plan.

A facilitator arranges experiences.

A teacher or lecturer disseminates information.

A facilitator evaluates based on the ability to apply skills.

A teacher or lecturer evaluates based on repeating facts and information.

In this chapter we begin by identifying strategies for creating a climate for learning and participation. Then we present eight facilitation methods that are effective for all phases of lifeguard training, including water drills. Last, but not least, we review facilitator questioning skills and ask you to apply a self-assessment tool.

Creating a Positive Climate for Learning and Participation

The learning climate refers to all of the conditions that affect your students' perceptions of the training. If a climate is perceived to be bad (demeaning, a waste of time, unproductive, boring, uncomfortable, and so on), learning will occur more slowly or not at all. If a climate is perceived to be good (supportive, comfortable, enjoyable, productive, worthwhile, engaging, and so on), learning and participation will be enhanced. Consider the following three elements of climate:

1. What you do before the course begins
2. The physical environment
3. How you greet and engage your students

Before the Course

To help create a good learning climate, consider taking these actions before the course starts:

- Send a welcome letter to students before training begins. Explain the goals of the training and what to expect, along with a reminder about times, dates, and directions. This letter will immediately begin to set the tone for your training.
- Distribute student texts and reading assignments.
- Conduct an orientation meeting for parents. This can go a long way toward setting the climate, especially for your younger students. A sample parent orientation outline is included in the appendix.

Physical Environment

The physical environment may be the most difficult element for you to control, especially if you are training outdoors. If conditions are not ideal, acknowledge that you recognize your students' discomfort and are sorry, identifying what you can and cannot control. When possible, share their discomfort. For example, if your students are expected to be in and out of the water in chilly conditions, they could become discouraged if you stand on the deck in a warm, dry parka. Experiencing the conditions with your students will help establish your credibility as a facilitator.

Other outdoor conditions you should consider are sun angles, temperature, and insects.

- Position yourself so that the sun shines toward you and is at your students' backs. This keeps the sun out of their eyes.
- Adjust the duration of outdoor and in-water training activity if the conditions are either too cold or too warm. Continuously monitor your students for signs of hypothermia or hyperthermia; if you see signs of either, immediately stop the activity and provide care.
- Keep insect repellent and sting care supplies readily available in case insects become a problem.

How you arrange the physical environment can also have an impact on the learning experience. Seating arrangements can determine the level of participation you can expect from your students. Figures 2.1-2.3 illustrate how adjusting the seating arrangement can encourage more student participation.

Figure 2.1 Worst arrangement. Arrangements like this that separate the instructor or facilitator from the students discourage students' participation and active involvement. Arrangements with the instructor behind a table, facing the students, and students behind tables create a double barrier.

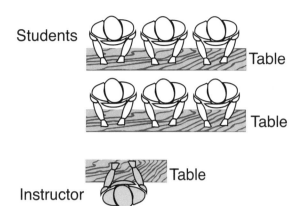

Students

Table

Table

Instructor

Table

Figure 2.2 Better arrangement. Arrangements that place the instructor at the head of the class but allow for better exchange between students facilitate a medium level of involvement.

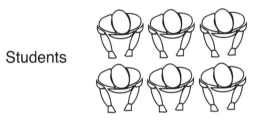

Students

Instructor

Instructor

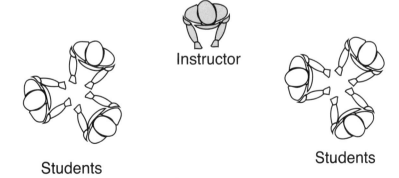

Students

Students

Figure 2.3 Best arrangement. Arrangements that arrange students into small groups or incorporate the instructor into the larger group facilitate high involvement. Using a series of small tables, or no tables, allows the arrangement to be flexible and easily changed to accommodate activities that may need open floor space.

When you arrange students into pairs or groups, use some of these easy, entertaining ways to break them up:

Playing cards. Pull from a deck of plastic-coated playing cards the same number of cards as the number of students in the class. Evenly distribute the number of each suit. For example, if you have 12 students, pull out three hearts, three clubs, three diamonds, and three spades from the deck. Deal one card to each student. The students holding a particular suit form one group. A similar technique is to write the name of each student on a card, shuffle, and deal into groups.

Candy break. Pass around a bucket of different types of candy. Students divide into groups based on the candy chosen (e.g., peppermints, butterscotch, toffee). A similar technique is to pass around a bag of M&M's, presorted by color into the number of students you want in each group.

Preferences. Divide students into two groups based on answers to questions about the type of car they drive, music they prefer, and so on. Continue the process until the groups are even. For example, say, "I'm going to give you two choices. Move to my right if you drive a truck, to my left if you drive a car. Move to my right if your car has four-wheel drive, to my left if it doesn't. Move to my right if your car is blue, black, or gold; move to my left if your car is white, red, or yellow."

Sit or stand. Tell everyone to find a partner. In each pair one person sits and the other stands. Those standing become one group, those sitting become the second group. Or, tell everyone to stand and cross their arms. Those with the right arm on top become one group, those with the left arm on top become the second group. A similar technique is to ask students to fold their hands together and separate into groups based on which thumb is on top—right or left.

Leaders. Pick four leaders (or the number of leaders for the number of groups you want). Pick the leaders using criteria such as those who live closest (or farthest) from the training site, those with the most pets (including fish), those who exercise the most, those who watch the most (or least) TV, and so on. The leaders stand side by side. The other students line up behind the leader of their choice, but each column must contain the same number of students. The groups are determined by which students are in corresponding rows (i.e., all the students who are last in the column become a group and so on).

Handshake roundup. Students form a circle and count off by twos. All number twos step into the circle and turn to face out. Those on the outside of the circle face in. Start clapping or turn on music. When the clapping or music starts, the inside circle walks clockwise, and the outside circle walks counterclockwise. Students shake hands with each person they pass, alternating right hand and left hand. When the music or clapping stops, new partner groups have been formed. This activity can also be conducted in the water, and it is a good lead-up into organized water drills for rescue skills practice.

Greeting and Engaging Students

It's been said that you never have a second chance to make a first impression. Your students will begin to form an impression of your training within the first few minutes. If you immediately create an emotionally satisfying climate, you will be off to a great start. Failure to do so can sabotage your facilitation efforts and take hours to overcome. To make your students feel at ease, feel valued, and believe that the training session is likely to be valuable do the following:

- Start on time.

- Begin with an activity right away that gets your students moving and involved. Paperwork and other "housekeeping" tasks can wait. Students who expected to come to a class to watch videos and listen to an instructor read out of a book will quickly realize that this course is different; those who expected to be involved will realize their expectations. All students will begin to see that participation and involvement are part of the program. Icebreaker activities, such as "Have You Ever" and "Name Toss," which are detailed in block plan 1, are excellent ways to establish the learning climate and also accomplish training goals within the first five minutes of class. Interaction, creative thinking, teamwork, and fun are all benefits of icebreakers.

- Let students know what to expect. Students will have a much greater level of emotional safety if they feel informed about your objectives and expectations. Create ground rules that help maintain a safe environment and keep things running smoothly. The following are examples of ground rules: We will start and end on time, we will speak one at a time, you will take charge of your own learning, we will apply sunscreen (if outdoors), we will enter the water feetfirst only, and we will not enter the water unless a lifeguard is in place.

You've seen how you can set the stage for effective learning. Now let's turn to facilitation techniques you can use to guide learning.

Facilitation Techniques

The following techniques are effective for training lifeguards:

- Debriefing
- Demonstration
- Role-play
- Scenarios
- Lecturettes
- Small-group discussions
- Experiential activities
- Drills

Debriefing

Debriefing is learning through reflection, and it is a critical component in the learning process for adults. A debriefing should be the last component of every training technique. Your role in debriefing is to guide your students through a reflective process until they discover the learning that took place and that they can use that learning to make beneficial changes. Depending on the training activity, the debriefing may be short, or it may take longer than the activity itself. To conduct a debriefing, ask questions such as these:

- Did you feel that was successful? Why?
- What did you do when _____?
- How did you feel when _____?
- What was challenging for you?
- What did your group do when_____?
- How did you handle_____?
- Did you expect _____?
- What needs to happen for you to succeed?
- What will you do to make sure _____doesn't happen again?
- What was the highlight for you?
- What do you think this activity was designed to teach?
- How will you use this learning?

During a debriefing, avoid the following:

- Offering answers
- Comparing one student's actions to another's
- Giving insincere praise or undue criticism
- Accepting only one right way, even if another method meets the objective

Demonstration

A demonstration presents a method for doing something. Demonstrations are useful for the motor skills, such as aquatic rescues and CPR, that are part of lifeguard training. You may be the demonstrator, or it may be someone else who can perform the skill correctly. To focus your students' attention on the performance, avoid talking and explaining while a demonstration is taking place for the first time. You don't want to create a situation where your students are torn between watching or listening. When the demonstration is complete, talk through the action steps to communicate your specific teaching points.

Also avoid demonstrations using only gestures or partial movements. For example, simulating opening an airway on an imaginary person rather than demonstrating on a person or a manikin* as you talk through the steps does not provide your students the modeling they need. If you can't demonstrate the entire skill the way you want your students to perform it, it's usually better to not demonstrate it at all.

When conducting a land demonstration for a skill that will be performed in the water, be sure to use a rescue tube and simulate body positions as close to the way they will occur in the water as possible. When you demonstrate an underwater skill on land, have two students hold each end of the rescue tube above your head to simulate the surface of the water and where the rescue tube would be positioned during the rescue.

Position yourself so that all your students can see your demonstration. You may want to repeat the demonstration from more than one angle, for example, from a front view and then a side view. Here is an example of how to conduct a rear-rescue demonstration:

* The spelling *manikin* is used when referring to a CPR training simulation device.

- Position your students so that they can see you.
- State the objective of the demonstrated skill. For example, say, "For your own safety, it is important to keep the rescue tube between you and a distressed swimmer or drowning victim at all times and then to keep both you and the other person up on the tube so that you can breathe. I'm going to demonstrate how to do this when approaching someone from the rear."
- Position yourself at the side of the pool, or in the lifeguard stand, wearing your rescue tube. Hold the rescue tube across your chest with the strap gathered. Yell out the scan, target, assess, alert, rescue steps as you prepare to use a compact jump to enter the water and approach the drowning victim.
- Perform a rear rescue.
- Debrief the activity. Ask your students questions such as "Was that rescue successful?" *Yes.* "Why?" *Because the rescue tube was between the rescuer and the other person, both heads were up so that they could breathe, and progress was made to the side.* "Where did I keep the rescue tube?" *The rescue tube was across your chest.* "What did I do just before I made contact?" *You turned your head to prevent injury.* "How did I reach around the person?" *You reached under the arms.*
- Summarize key teaching points. *(Keep the tube across your chest. Turn your head before contact. Reach under the arms.)*
- Demonstrate again from a different angle.

After a demonstration, have your students practice the skill and give them feedback. After practice, debrief the activity with your students by discussing how easy or difficult it was, what they discovered, and how the skill might be used in the future.

Role-Play

During role-playing, a small group of students acts out a real-life situation. The actions are not scripted, but instead develop into an engaging way of presenting information and stimulating discussion. Role-play is effective when you train lifeguards how to administer first aid, enforce rules, manage crowds, deal with patrons, and exhibit professional behavior.

One benefit of role-playing is that all students participate by either acting or observing. Role-playing allows students to experience the consequences of their actions as well as possible reactions from others. Role-playing can also help change attitudes. For role-playing to be effective, you should do the following:

- Clearly describe the scene so that both observers and participants understand their roles and the situation.
- Observe the role-play and stop it if it gets off task.
- Debrief by thanking the role-play actors and asking how they felt in the roles. Elicit reactions and comments from the observers, but protect the actors from negative comments. Ask the observers to frame comments in the form of suggestions on how the situation might have been handled differently. Summarize learning points.

Scenarios

A scenario is similar to role-playing—students assume a role, such as a rescuer or drowning victim—but they actually perform specific actions rather than act them out. For example, a role play of a rescue scene might be conducted in a classroom while a scenario of a rescue scene would be conducted in the pool, with students positioned to respond from locations that mirror real life. Scenario training is critical to developing a lifeguard's ability to put together all types of learning—knowledge, skills, and application of learning and attitude—to effectively manage an emergency situation. A scenario is a reality test and allows all students to participate through either experiencing, thinking, self-critiquing, or critiquing others.

A well-constructed scenario allows students to perform in as close to a real-life situation as possible without worrying about the consequences of their actions. A scenario is your best opportunity as an instructor to observe your students using all types of learning. If a student cannot reasonably perform a skill during a scenario, it is unlikely that he or she will be able to perform it on the job.

Scenarios provide immediate feedback because students are able to discover and react on their own. Further debriefing will help clarify for your students what they learned and how this knowledge relates to them and can be used in the future. Follow these steps to conduct a scenario:

- When possible, place all necessary equipment and people where they would be located in a real situation. This step is crucial for evaluating the effectiveness of logistics as well as performance.
- Identify the roles of the students in the scenario (e.g., primary rescuer and backup lifeguard).
- Introduce the goals and rules and the safety considerations, such as refraining from breathing into the "drowning victim" or pressing down during compressions.
- Facilitate the scenario by providing cues after actions are performed, such as "You do not see the chest rise," to keep the situation going.
- Debrief the scenario by first asking the participants to evaluate themselves. Then summarize the learning points and relate how this information can be used in the future.

Lecturettes

A lecturette is a short, concise lecture. It is best used to provide specific information that will form the foundation for the next activity. For example, a lecturette on the function and use of an automated external defibrillator (AED) is appropriate before practicing with the AED. A lecturette is *not* a one-way communication device, like a traditional lecture. A lecturette has an organized structure, but you engage your students in the process by asking questions that prompt them to supply some of the information. For example, rather than saying, "You must shave the chest before applying the pads," ask, "What do you think would happen if I put the pads on this person's hairy chest?" *The pads would not stick.* "So what has to happen?" *We need to shave the chest and make sure we have a razor in the responder bag.*

After each question your role will be to confirm right answers and to correct misinformation. This acknowledges what your students already know while you present new information. Avoid letting one or two students monopolize the question-and-answer exchange. Randomly pick students to provide the answers, and try to involve as many as possible.

Small-Group Discussions

A small-group discussion allows students to share experiences, develop ideas, and solve problems. Small-group discussions can develop group cohesion, teamwork, critical thinking, and problem-solving skills. Participants learn from each other and through reflection on their own experience. To facilitate small-group discussion follow these guidelines:

- Divide your students into small groups.
- Clearly introduce a specific task or topic to be discussed. Providing specific directions in your introduction will help focus your students' attention. For example, asking students to discuss prevention may not be as effective as asking students to discuss ways to reduce injury on specific play features.
- Provide a deadline. Keep it short enough to maintain interest, but long enough that each student has a chance to participate.
- Assign or let each group designate a facilitator who will keep the group on task, a recorder who will write down the ideas generated, and a reporter who will summarize the group's findings for the class.
- Begin the discussion. Move among the groups to answer questions and make sure that no one is left out because others are dominating the discussion.
- Reconvene all of the groups for a presentation by the reporters.
- Summarize the common points or themes that the groups discovered or created.
- Debrief to determine what students learned and how they plan to use it.

Experiential Activities

An activity should result in a specific outcome. Experiential activities refer to those that allow students to arrive at the outcome on their own, rather than being told or shown. With thought and creativity, almost any element of lifeguard training can be developed into an experiential activity. For example, lifeguards must understand prevention strategy. Rather than using a show-and-tell technique—this is our safety equipment; here are the pool rules—think about how your students could discover prevention strategies for themselves. One method is the Walk-About experiential activity in StarGuard block plan 2, although there could be numerous others. If you evaluate each aspect of your training by asking "How can my students learn this for themselves?" you will be able to develop new and engaging training activities.

Drills

Drills, whether on land or in the water, are usually the most effective method of providing a hands-on learning experience for large groups of students at the same time. Drills are usually conducted with the entire class separated into pairs or small groups; therefore, you must have techniques for reorganizing your students quickly and effectively (as described in the Physical Environment section). Properly planned drills meet the following criteria:

- They maximize the space available.
- They provide the most number of turns for each student or most opportunity to practice.
- They are safe and appropriate for the skill you are teaching.
- They have a purpose, and you have identified the outcome your students should achieve.

Conducting drills in the water requires additional organization and planning. Once your students are in the water, it will be more difficult for you to communicate, especially to the whole class at once. To make the most of your water time, do the following:

- Keep your students moving and involved. Set up drills that keep the most students active at a time, with minimal wait time between turns.
- Design drills so that your students practice with many different people and body types.
- Eliminate time wasters from your drills. For example, once your students have mastered the entry and approach stroke, eliminate the time spent swimming out to the simulated drowning victim and then swimming back and climbing out by having students start from, and remain in, the water during the drill.
- Demonstrate on land, demonstrate in the water, and then let students complete several trials (preferably five) of the same skill before introducing a new skill (figure 2.4).

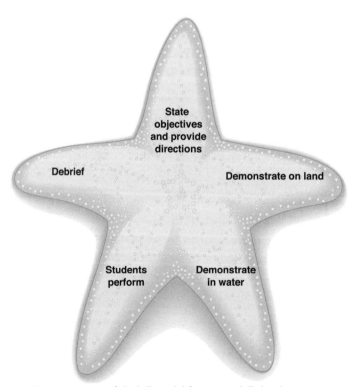

Figure 2.4 Starfish drill model for water skill development.

• Provide brief performance feedback to each student individually after his or her turn. Debrief the group as a whole after every student has had one turn. Provide specific teaching tips that will help improve the most common performance errors you observe, and then continue the drill.

• Set up experiences so that your students will figure out how to perform a skill on their own (with your facilitation), rather than being told how to perform. For example, when introducing the front rescue of a conscious drowning victim, you might say, "When you approach a victim from the front, there are three objectives: (1) to keep control of your rescue tube and keep it between yourself and the drowning victim, (2) to avoid body-to-body contact, and (3) to keep your head and the drowning victim's head above water while you get back to the side. Let me see you make a rescue that meets these objectives." In most cases, your students will, on the first try, perform an effective rescue that meets the objectives. Because your students have mastered the basics, the feedback you provide from this point forward can focus on the finer performance points. When teaching a skill that involves specific steps or technique, a demonstration provides a picture of the performance you expect.

The first step in planning drills is to make sure that all the equipment you need is readily available. Next plan how many people will be in each group for each drill and which technique you will use to separate your students into these groups. Finally, give students clear directions on where to go, how many people should be in each group, how the drill will be conducted, and how many times they should practice before moving or changing. Suggested drill formations include the following:

Front-line drill. The front-line drill (figure 2.5) is ideal for providing students with a lot of practice with various body types in a short amount of time. Divide students into pairs, forming a line of rescuers and a line of drowning victims. Student rescuers start from on deck or in the water. Signal the start of each rescue or allow the student pairs to work at their own pace. Students perform the skill two times each,

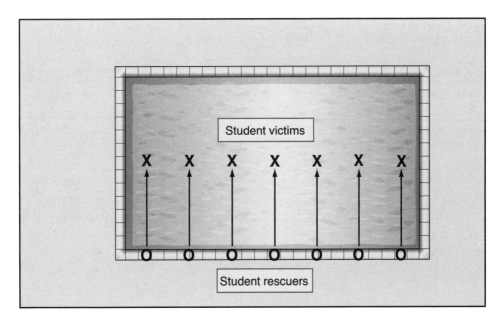

Figure 2.5 Front-line drill.

being both the rescuer and the victim. The victim on the far right then moves to a rescuer's position and the rest of the students move accordingly. Another option is to rotate just the victims or just the rescuers; after several turns, the rescuers become victims and the victims become rescuers.

Wave drill. The wave drill (figure 2.6) is similar to the front-line drill, except that you signal the entry of each rescuer. Stagger the starts, giving start commands a few seconds apart. Choose this drill if you want to observe the performance of each student individually.

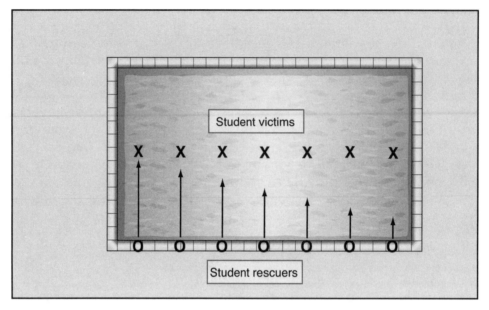

Figure 2.6   Wave drill.

Corner drill. Choose the corner drill (figure 2.7) when you want to move students through a skill practice quickly, when you want to observe each student's performance individually, or when you do not have a lot of pool space. Divide students into two even lines along the deck on opposite sides of one corner of the pool. One line is designated rescuers, the other drowning victims. On your command, the first drowning victim moves away from the wall into the center of the corner and exhibits drowning symptoms. The next person in the rescuer line makes the rescue. The victim goes to the end of the rescuer line and the rescuer to the end of the victim line. To keep this drill moving quickly, have the next victim swim out to position as the previous victim is swimming to the end of the rescuer line.

So far we've discussed teaching techniques, but the most important concept to keep in mind as you teach is that you are not just instructing students but instead are facilitating their learning.

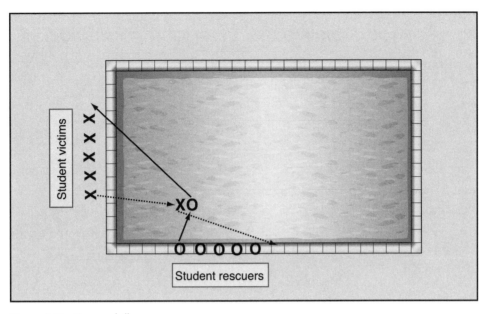

Figure 2.7   Corner drill.

Obtaining Feedback

A big part of being a facilitator is knowing how to ask the right questions. Have you ever been in a situation in which everyone in the room stays silent when you ask, "Does anyone have any questions?" at the end of a training session? It could be that there are no questions, but it is more likely that your students don't want to look dumb in front of others, or have already emotionally left the room and are ready to bolt out of the door. Instead, try asking the following:

- What do I need to clarify?
- What have I forgotten?
- How can I help you use this information?

These "I" questions shift the responsibility for not knowing something to you, and your students will be much more likely to respond. When a student requests clarification, repeat his or her question for the whole group so that your answer can be related to what was asked. Always try to validate and affirm the question when you repeat it. For example, start with "That's a great question; the question is . . ." or "It's interesting that you ask that; Tim posed the question . . ."

Asking open-ended questions is another effective method for engaging students. These questions cannot be answered by yes or no and usually start with the words "What do you," "Why do you think," "How will you," "How can you," "What if," "What has been," or "What are some."

Are You a Skilled Instructor and Facilitator?

Read the following statements and note how many apply to you, or if they identify areas that need improvement. Commit to strengthening at least one or two before your next training session.

I know the subject matter.

I know my students.

I am confident and fully prepared.

I am just nervous enough to stay alert and "up."

I respect differences of opinion and lifestyle.

I recognize my biases and know my hot buttons and remain professional when challenged.

I am culturally sensitive.

I am inclusive.

I am enthusiastic and lively.

I have a relaxed posture and use meaningful gestures and expressions.

I make remarks that are clear and easy to remember.

I understand group dynamics.

I understand that students learn in different ways.

I am flexible.

I am open to new ideas.

I am compassionate.

I share relevant personal experience.

I meet and greet students when they arrive.

I arrange the classroom to encourage participation.

I ask open-ended questions.

I prefer to sit in a circle with the students instead of standing up front.

I encourage students to try out new ideas.

I dress in appropriate, professional attire.

I manage time effectively.

I try to create an excitement-filled atmosphere.

I vary activities.

I paraphrase and summarize discussions.

I mingle with students during breaks.

I can sense when the group is energized or fatigued, interested or disinterested.

I enjoy giving praise and recognition.

I listen with interest.

I am approachable.

I involve those who are holding back.

I often redirect questions to other students.

I always learn from my students.

I constantly seek to improve my facilitation skills.

3

Instructors' Challenges

Every instructor knows that conducting lifeguard courses is highly dynamic—no two proceed exactly the same. The curriculum is the only constant; the teaching environment and the students both can create new and challenging situations. In this chapter we explore strategies to meet these challenges, starting with how to minimize problems when coteaching with other instructors. We also consider how to meet the challenges of working with a diverse group of students and then move into strategies for dealing with difficult students and less-than-ideal teaching conditions.

Coteaching

Coteaching refers to multiple instructors conducting a StarGuard course together. Coteaching provides benefits, but it also presents challenges that you must consider if you are to be successful. Coteaching can help you by allowing you to do the following:

- Reduce the stress and fatigue level by sharing responsibility.
- Learn from the other instructors.
- Gain feedback on personal performance from another instructor.
- Keep each other on track, accountable, and excited.
- Complement each other and focus on each other's strengths.
- Share the triumph of a great course.

Coteaching can benefit the students by providing the following:

- Variety in delivery
- More performance monitoring (While one instructor presents, the other instructor can observe students.)
- Smaller groups
- Improved evaluation through several assessments rather than just one

- Lessons in teamwork and professional respect by watching interactions between instructors

The relationship between co-instructors is important. When instructors have similar experience levels, coteaching works best when all cooperate, share, defer to each other, and show mutual respect. When one instructor has significantly more experience, the roles of the co-instructors become those of mentor and apprentice. In both situations effective planning and clear expectations for everyone will help prevent misunderstandings that could detract from the learning experience. The following are tips to ensure that working with co-instructors goes smoothly:

- Decide ahead of time how disputes will be resolved so that disagreements don't occur in front of students.
- In your precourse planning, identify each instructor's strengths so that the human resources are used to the best advantage.
- Determine ahead of time who will open class, close class, make announcements, take the lead for an activity, and so on as well as where each instructor will stand, conduct drills, and store equipment.
- Once the training session begins, frequently evaluate how the course is going and make adjustments.
- Show respect for each other and be flexible. Rivalry and personal pettiness can sabotage the best efforts at coteaching.

Potential sources of conflict are numerous when coteaching, but you can avoid all of them by sharing a "big picture" vision of the course objectives, respecting each others' differences, and committing to professional excellence. Most coteaching frustrations come from a *perceived* inequality in regard to effort, knowledge, attitude, or respect. Your perceptions may or may not be correct, so keep the lines of communication open. Table 3.1 presents some common coteaching frustrations and suggested solutions.

Knowing how to handle differences between the instructors you work with is an important skill. It also helps you relate to the different needs of your students.

Managing Students' Diversity

The students who enroll in StarGuard courses are diverse in many ways. We often think of diversity as it relates to gender, race, and cultural backgrounds. However, the concept of diversity in a learning environment is much broader. Your students may differ in age, physical ability, sexual orientation, religious and political beliefs, education levels, and learning ability. They may also exhibit differences in motivation and commitment and have different levels of responsibility and influence. For example, some of your students may be rookie lifeguards, while others may be lifeguard supervisors or facility managers.

You must be sensitive to these differences and work to ensure that your training sessions are free from discrimination, harassment, prejudice, and abusive behavior. You should anticipate that diverse groups of students will have different learning needs and, to the extent practical, prepare to meet these needs. General guidelines for managing diversity include the following, which were adapted from *Teaching a Diverse Student Body, Second Edition,* published by the Teaching Resource Center at the University of Virginia in 2004.

Table 3.1

Problem	Solutions
"She went over her time, and I didn't have enough time to conduct my activity."	Don't steal each other's time; watch the clock and plan accordingly. Plan transitions to move from activity to activity in an organized manner.
"When he's done with his activity he disappears."	Stay involved even when another instructor has the whole group. You can learn from watching others teach, and you can be available to help or to monitor student progress.
"I did all the work ahead of time. All she did was show up to teach."	Share the preclass preparation responsibilities as well as postclass cleanup and paperwork.
"He was supposed to bring the equipment, but forgot."	Stay on top of details and take responsibility for what you have been asked to do.
"She took my ideas and passed them off as her own."	Ask permission before presenting someone else's ideas, examples, or techniques. Taking credit for someone else's work creates a difficult working relationship.
"He went off on a tangent that ate up time and didn't accomplish anything."	Stick with the agenda.
"She put me down (contradicted me, yelled at me, and so on) in front of the students."	Keep all disagreements out of earshot and sight of students. If a correction must be made in front of the group, handle it in a manner that does not show disrespect for the other instructor or make the other instructor look weak.
"He butts in and takes over in the middle of my activity."	Know when to take a supportive role, and only get involved when asked.
"She gets mad because we're not doing it her way."	Be fully cooperative, even when you are upset about the method or believe there is an inequality in the workload.
"He doesn't have control over his students. He's more interested in being their buddy than their instructor, and I have to be the bad guy."	Share the responsibility for class management, and make sure you're not contributing to the problem through your own attitude or actions.

Gender and Appearance

- Don't overlook capable but quiet students of either sex. Encourage participation of all students, not just those who always answer questions.
- Give male and female students equal attention when providing feedback or debriefing. Don't ask female students to perform activities you would not request of male students or vice versa.
- If you observe students making sexist remarks, whether in front of the whole class or in smaller groups, address the students and tell them that such remarks are inappropriate and do not further the purposes of the course.
- Don't comment on your students' physical appearance.
- Maintain the highest level of professionalism in and out of the classroom. Remarks considered denigrating of women or men, even when intended as humor, could constitute sexual harassment.

Race and Ethnicity

- Learn how to pronounce your students' names.
- Ask about your students' interests and experiences so that you get to know them as individuals rather than merely members of the group.
- Don't make assumptions about students based on what you believe their racial or ethnic-related experiences, needs, or abilities are.
- Don't assume the identity or racial affiliation of a student based on his or her physical appearance.
- If you need to discuss problems, approach students one on one rather than singling them out in class.
- Pay equal attention to all students.
- Be aware of the great diversity within an ethnic group or community.
- If students are Native Americans, be sensitive to their expressed tribal affiliation. For example, their identity and pride may come from being identified as Cherokee or Navajo.
- Don't make assumptions regarding students' language capabilities based on their ethnic background.
- Use the terms white (not Caucasian), Asian (not Oriental), Native American (not Indian), African American or black, and Native Alaskan (not Eskimo).
- If there is a language barrier, speak in clear, direct sentences and avoid jargon or slang.

Age

- Include older students in all training activities so that they feel a part of the group.
- Understand that older students are in class to learn from you, so their presence should not be intimidating.
- Take advantage of the life experience as well as the different perspectives older students bring to your training.

Sexual Orientation

- Don't assume that all students in a class are heterosexual.
- React firmly to disparaging remarks made at any time. Presenting a "respect for your classmates" contract or ground rule at the beginning of class helps.
- Do not assume that all people who are HIV positive are gay or that only gay people engage in activities that put themselves and others at risk of HIV.

Religion and Political Beliefs

- Assume that your students have diverse religious and political views.
- Accommodate students' important religious holidays.
- Never criticize or joke about a religion or a religious or political belief.

Special Physical or Medical Needs

- Assume that your students can perform all skills unless they inform you otherwise. Always address a student with disabilities directly, not solely through an interpreter or caretaker.

- Ask a student with disabilities privately what things you can do to facilitate learning.
- Know what a student is unable to do and plan alternatives ahead of time.
- Adapt to the needs of a student with disabilities without lowering course standards.
- When covering a topic in emergency care dealing with illness or disease, assume that this topic may affect some students personally.
- Reward achievements with relevant praise and offer critiques when a student with a disability could improve his or her performance, just as you would for any other student.
- Students with disabilities generally do not enjoy praise that is based on their disability rather than on their ability.
- Make reasonable accommodation for skills performance when students with disabilities are unable to perform at the same level as the rest of the class (e.g., arranging for the assistance of a sign interpreter, modifying skills sessions).

Learning Styles

- Understand that students are diverse in the way they prefer to learn.
- Students that are auditory learners like to listen and learn from what they hear.
- Students that are visual learners like to be shown and learn from what they see.
- Students that are kinesthetic learners like to perform a skill and learn from what they do.

Learning Disability

- Take the initiative. If you notice that a student has a learning problem, talk to the student privately.
- Present material in a variety of ways: visually, verbally, role-playing, and so on.
- Allow alternative testing formats and extended time when appropriate.
- Avoid looking annoyed when a student asks a question you have just answered.
- Keep students' attention by modulating your voice and gesturing to emphasize significant points.
- Help students to organize, synthesize, and apply information.
- Consider putting a statement in your course registration materials encouraging students with special learning needs to discuss them with you.
- Build rapport with the student who has a learning disability and establish a one-on-one relationship with him or her. Ask questions to find out about interests or talents the student may possess.
- Do not try to spare students with learning disabilities from embarrassment by ignoring them.
- Look for opportunities in which a student with a learning disability can demonstrate what he or she knows or can do in order to enhance the student's confidence.

- Help the student with learning disabilities by targeting the student's area of difficulty and suggesting a strategy for compensation.

Adapted, by permission, from D. Little, 2004, *Teaching a diverse student body*, 2nd ed. (Charlottesville, VA: University of Virginia).

Just as you can expect your students to be from diverse backgrounds, you also can expect to encounter students whose attitudes make it more difficult to prepare them to become responsible lifeguards. The following section discusses some of the types of students you may find in your classes.

Managing Difficult Students

If a student is not fully engaged and participating in your class, look for the underlying cause. The cause may be outside your control, as when a student is hungry, tired, or dealing with personal problems. However, the cause may be your teaching methods and the student's behavior a symptom.

A solution may be to switch to an activity that uses a teaching method that appeals to your difficult student's learning style. For example, if you are presenting information verbally, the student may not be an auditory learner and may respond better to an activity that presents information visually or kinesthetically through a hands-on activity.

A student's underlying motivations or personality traits may pose additional challenges to you as an instructor. Some of the most common types of students you may have to deal with include the following:

Stud duck. A stud duck believes that lifeguarding is all about the heroics of the rescue, physical skills, and emergency care prowess. Your biggest challenge will be to help this person realize the importance of prevention, surveillance, and professionalism, especially during the slow times when there's not much action.

Patch collector. A patch collector takes training for the sake of building up a resume of certifications, and he or she sometimes has a "been there, done that" attitude of complacency. Your biggest challenge will be to keep this student motivated to learn, grow, and explore new ways of doing things, rather than just going through the motions to achieve the certification card.

Clueless. This student has adequate skills and knowledge, but lacks the passion or desire to understand the *why* of lifeguarding. Your biggest challenge will be to instill a sense of what the consequences of remaining clueless could be, especially if he or she gets a job at a facility that lacks effective leadership and a risk management system.

Sun god or goddess. This student believes a fantasy about what the job of a lifeguard entails. He or she envisions being able to get a tan and get paid for it and views lifeguarding as something to do until getting a "real" job. Your biggest challenge will be similar to the one you face with the clueless student as well convincing this person of the importance of sun protection and professionalism.

Dependent. This student does not function independently. The parents do everything for him or her—filling out the registration form, calling in sick, or asking for special considerations. Your biggest challenge will be to get the parents to understand the level of responsibility the student must assume in a lifeguarding position and that the ability to function independently and be accountable is crucial to that role.

Talker. This student tends to be a know-it-all and monopolizes the class. This may be because he or she is well informed and naturally engaging, or this student may be a show-off and make minimal contributions. Usually the group dynamics will rein in a talker, but you can take steps to make sure this person does not take time away from other students. When in the group, paraphrase what this student says and then move on, or acknowledge the student's contribution and tactfully say something like, "That's an interesting point, and now let's see what the rest of the class thinks." Another strategy is to give the talker a task to complete that takes him or her away from the group for a while.

Expert. These students are often the "real deal" (in contrast to a talker) and can be a tremendous resource to you. However, left unappreciated, the expert can become bored and possibly distract other students. When you identify a talented student, approach him or her and ask for a higher level of involvement and assistance in helping other students.

Challenger. Encourage your students to be involved and ask questions, especially those that are legitimate attempts to gain information. However, some students use questioning to disrupt or challenge. He or she questions everything you say or propose and seems to challenge your credibility. Such a student might also get off onto topics that have little to do with the learning objective and eat up valuable training time. To deal with this type of student, bounce the questions back to the group or say that you'll get back to the questions at a more appropriate time. If the situation is extremely disruptive, consider talking privately with the student and asking for cooperation.

You may also encounter challenging situations when you pose a question to your students. Let's look at some examples.

Dealing With Questions

In an ideal learning environment, the facilitator and students engage in a lively exchange of ideas back and forth, usually as the result of some form of questioning. Sometimes, however, the process of questioning creates potentially difficult situations for an instructor.

1. *You've asked a question and a student gives a wrong answer.* Rather than simply correcting the student, respond with another question that leads the student to the right answer. Or ask the class, "How does everyone else feel about this answer?" and get a dialog going about the topic, redirecting attention away from the student.

2. *You don't understand a student's answer.* Restate what you understood and let the student provide additional information to clarify. Or state that you didn't understand the answer and ask for rewording, for example, "I'm sorry, I didn't grasp your response. Could you give it to me again?" Another option is to ask the class for help in clarifying the student's response.

3. *A student answers in a slow, rambling, or off-topic manner.* You may need to tactfully interrupt the student, paraphrase the key point that is on topic, and redirect

to another student. For example, saying, "I think I understand where you're going with this, and you do agree that _____. Susie, can you summarize for us?"

4. *No one answers the question.* There could be several reasons for this: The question was poorly worded and not understood, the students may not know the answer, or you have not yet established a learning climate. Consider rephrasing the question and asking it in another way, or answering it yourself and moving on.

5. *A student asks an irrelevant or distracting question.* Redirect the question to a "parking lot" where you will address it at another time. For example, you could respond with, "John, that's an interesting question that I'd like to explore with you after we complete this activity. Let's put it in the parking lot and discuss it right before the lunch break."

6. *A student asks a question to which you don't know the answer.* You have two choices in this situation: Admit that you don't have the answer, but state that you will find out and get back to the student, or redirect the question to the class to see if they can establish an answer. Your credibility will suffer if you attempt to bluff your way through or partially answer a question.

Besides tough questions, problems with the physical environment that make teaching and learning uncomfortable will challenge you from time to time. The next section offers suggestions for handling these.

Handling Difficult Environments

When teaching at an indoor aquatic facility, you know you can expect it to be hot, humid, and possibly noisy and crowded. When teaching at an outdoor aquatic facility, you are likely to face a variety of uncontrollable conditions. For example, it could be hot (or cold), windy, noisy, or buggy. You should anticipate unexpected inadequacies in your teaching environment. When problems disrupt your training routine, how you handle these circumstances will determine the attitude of your students. Try the following approaches:

- Encourage your students to adjust, and adjust your training activity according to the situation.
- Focus on the positive.
- Let your students know that you understand their discomfort or frustration.
- Avoid placing blame on anyone for the situations or conditions. Deal privately with the decision maker who can resolve the problem.
- If possible, relocate.
- In a worst-case scenario, cancel and reschedule the session.

If you deal with uncomfortable conditions well, you can develop mutual cooperation and acceptance; however, if you don't, you are likely to create resentment and anger in your students. Whatever the circumstances, take a positive, problem-solving approach rather than an "Isn't it awful?" attitude.

4

Learning Online

Key technological developments provide new approaches for teaching and learning. Online (distance) learning through the use of the virtual environment of the Internet is one of the topics most talked about in academia today. The virtual-learning concept is being adopted in all forms of training, and lifeguarding is no exception. In this chapter we identify the advantages of learning online, followed by specific details about this option for the StarGuard course and the role of the StarGuard instructor in this process.

Before we examine the advantages, let's answer the fundamental question of "Does online training provide a good learning experience?" Like traditional learning, the experience depends on the quality of the course. Online training—when it is objective based, information rich, and interactive—can exceed the quality of classroom training.

A recent survey, *Entering the Mainstream: The Quality and Extent of Online Education in the United States, 2003 and 2004* (Allen and Seaman, 2004) compiled the responses of more than 1,100 colleges and universities. Some of the key findings include the following:

- More than 1.9 million students studied online in the fall of 2003.
- Schools expected the number of online students to grow to more than 2.6 million by the fall of 2004.
- Of schools offering online courses, 40.7 percent agree that "students are at least as satisfied" with their online courses as with traditional ones, 56.2 percent are neutral, and only 3.1 percent disagree.
- The majority of all schools (53.6 percent) agree that online education is critical to their long-term strategy.
- A majority of academic leaders believe that online learning quality is already equal to or superior to face-to-face instruction.

Advantages of Online Learning

Because lifeguarding has not only a knowledge component but also skill and attitude components, an approach that blends an online presentation with face-to-face instruction is necessary. In a blended course, the knowledge component is taught online and the other components are taught through face-to-face instruction. A blended course offers several advantages. During the online portion of the course the learner has the ability to do the following:

- Learn anywhere, any time
- Work at his or her own pace
- Master details
- Repeat or continually review course content
- Obtain consistent, state-of-the-art content rather than rely on the varying skills of diverse instructors
- View a topic from different perspectives and in different ways (read, write, watch video, listen to audio)
- Demonstrate knowledge and how it could be applied to real-life problems
- Participate in knowledge assessment and documentation through review and quizzes

During the in-water, face-to-face instruction portion of the course the learner has the ability to do the following:

- Practice emergency care and aquatic rescue skills
- Practice surveillance strategies
- Integrate knowledge and skills by performing in rescue scenarios
- Participate in assessment and documentation of knowledge, performance, and attitude through a practical exam and a proctored written exam

Training lifeguards through a blended course offers the following advantages to an aquatic facility or training center:

- Cost savings
- Content standardization (The core training is uniform rather than based on delivery by diverse instructors.)
- Documentation of students' learning and successful completion
- Ability to update course materials quickly and keep current

The StarGuard online course focuses on sound learning methods rather than showy delivery. In other words, the attention is on principles of adult learning and application of learning strategies, not the "bells and whistles" of the computer. The course offers clear learning objectives, relevant examples, experiential activities, opportunities for practice, and feedback about performance. Let's look in more detail at how the StarGuard blended training option works.

StarGuard Blended Training

The StarGuard course delivered through the blended training format has two parts, the online experience and the in-water training. The first part consists of two online courses on emergency care and lifeguarding that are accessed through the Starfish Aquatics Education Center Web site, and the second part consists of face-to-face training with an instructor at an authorized Starfish Aquatics Institute training center. To participate in the blended training course, a student must have the following:

- Basic computer skills (keyboarding, browsing, navigating)
- Access to a computer with Internet connection
- Self-motivation and time management skills
- Ability to read English

To obtain StarGuard lifeguard certification, a student registers for the online courses through the Starfish Aquatics Education Center Web site and registers at a training center for the face-to-face instruction. Students register for the emergency care and lifeguarding online courses through the Starfish Aquatics Education Center Web site, following onscreen prompts.

Once a student has completed all of the online learning activities, he or she may click the Details link on the My Courses page in order to view the results of practice quizzes, e-mail a copy of the results, or print out a verification of successful completion to take to the training center in order to be admitted to the face-to-face training.

Training records for both the online courses and face-to-face training are maintained in an online database. This national registry is password protected, and it serves as a powerful resource to verify certification and track training requirements.

Upon completion of the online-study portion of the course, the lifeguard candidate should have an intellectual understanding of emergency care and lifeguarding techniques. He or she is now ready to interact face-to-face with a StarGuard instructor.

Role of the Instructor in Blended Training

To provide your students the best possible results from the StarGuard blended-learning course, you will be actively involved in two or three stages of the learning process:

- Precourse preparation and online learning
- In-water pool session and assessment
- Postcourse support

Precourse Preparation and Online Learning

The level of interaction you have with your students before the in-water course depends on your training center. If your training center employs the lifeguards going through the course, you probably will play an active role in helping your students prepare for the experience. Your students will experience a highly effective blending of the online and face-to-face delivery systems if you provide information about how the two parts of the StarGuard course work.

Students must take into account three factors to best absorb the material:

- Time management—when they will perform the course work, day, evening, weekends, and so on
- Location—where the computer for their course work will be located
- Scheduling—whether they will work on the course in several short chunks of time or fewer longer sessions

Ask your students to develop a list of questions and concerns and bring them to the face-to-face training. Conduct a parent orientation just as you would for a nonblended StarGuard course, and be prepared to discuss the blended format. If possible, demonstrate a section of one of the online courses.

If your training center does not employ the students that take your course, you will not have direct contact with them until they register for the face-to-face training. This usually occurs after they have completed the online courses.

In-Water Pool Session and Assessment

Before attending the in-water pool session, your students will have completed all of the knowledge objectives of the emergency care and lifeguarding online courses. The goal of the face-to-face session is for students to meet the skills, attitude, and performance objectives of the StarGuard course. During this session you will provide experiential activities to allow for skills practice, corrective feedback, scenario training, and performance evaluation in all five areas of the Starfish risk management model: prevention, surveillance, emergency care, aquatic rescue, and professionalism and personal safety. An outline of a sample block plan for the in-water portion of the blended StarGuard course is included in appendix G.

Postcourse Support

When the blended StarGuard course is complete, we hope that you will continue to offer support to your students. If your training center employs your students, this support will come through continued enhancement, or in-service, training and StarReview performance audits. If you do not have continued day-to-day contact with your students, you can provide support through e-mail reminders and messages. The following are suggested topics:

- Information on the Starfish Aquatics Institute Web site or intranet site
- Reminders to frequently review the content of the online study portion of the course
- Motivational quotes or short examples of specific best practices
- Invitations to workshops or seminars you are conducting
- Renewal date reminders

Facilitating
StarGuard Courses

PART II

© Human Kinetics

5

Instructor Certification and StarGuard Course Guidelines

This chapter outlines how to become an authorized StarGuard instructor, provides guidelines to follow when you teach a StarGuard course, and concludes with an overview of the suggested block plans.

To meet the requirements of the various regulatory agencies that approve national lifeguard training programs, you must follow certain guidelines when conducting a StarGuard course. Because of the continually changing regulatory environment, it's possible that the guidelines presented in this chapter have been superceded by new ones. To ensure that you follow the most current StarGuard course guidelines, check the *Starfish Training Center Administrative Manual (S-TCAM),* which is available through the training center with which you are affiliated. It is also possible that the StarGuard guidelines vary from your state's requirements. In such cases, follow your state regulations.

Becoming an Instructor

To become a StarGuard instructor, you must meet the prerequisites and requirements. You must agree to follow the course guidelines and understand that our students will assess you at the end of each course you teach. The Starfish Aquatics Institute will monitor the assessment results.

Instructor Prerequisites

Instructors are authorized to teach StarGuard courses and issue course completion certifications. A StarGuard instructor candidate must be at least 18 years of age and have successfully completed the StarGuard course within the past 12 months *or* hold a current certification in lifeguard or lifeguard instructor, including basic life support and CPR and first aid, from a nationally recognized training organization.

Instructor Requirements

To obtain instructor status, the first step is to successfully complete the StarGuard instructor development course. This course is designed to provide the necessary information, skills, and experiential education to successfully teach the StarGuard course. The components of this training include the following:

- Principles of adult learning
- How to create a nonthreatening environment that is conducive to learning
- Demonstration of basic life support skills by the instructor candidate
- Demonstration of water rescue and emergency management skills by the instructor candidate
- Principles of infection control, including proper decontamination of CPR manikins
- Facilitation of skill practice
- Use of audiovisual aids
- Orientation to training guidelines
- Discussion of course objectives
- Discussion of effective preparation, course management, and administrative procedures
- Discussion of student testing and evaluation
- Review of suggested block plans
- Facilitation of experiential activity
- Practice teaching assignment and evaluation

StarGuard instructor development courses are conducted through partnering with authorized training centers.

Once you have passed the instructor development course, you must sign an instructor agreement and become affiliated with an authorized training center. Instructor authorization is valid for three years, during which time you must maintain active status by teaching (or coteaching) at least once a year. If you maintain active status you can renew authorization through instructor seminars or other continuing-education opportunities. If you become inactive, you must complete the instructor development course in order to be recertified.

StarGuard instructors agree to follow the training guidelines set by the Starfish Aquatics Institute and, when teaching the emergency care courses, the guidelines set by the American Safety and Health Institute. These guidelines are presented in the most recent version of each agency's *Training Center and Administrative Manual (TCAM)*.

Instructor Responsibilities

The information contained in this instructor guide will help you meet the following objectives when you teach a StarGuard course:

- Dedicate the majority of class time to realistic team-based skill execution
- Instill in your students an understanding of the impact they can have in another's life and of the responsibilities of being a lifeguard

As an authorized instructor for the Starfish Aquatics Institute and American Safety and Health Institute, you are responsible for the following:

- Knowing the students you teach
- Planning and executing your plan to ensure a good learning experience for your students
- Knowing and executing strategies for managing your students in classroom and in-water environments
- Knowing the objectives for each course section and executing activities in an appropriate training area
- Knowing and executing the StarGuard course guidelines as outlined in the most recent version of the *Starfish Training Center Administrative Manual*, which may be different from those presented in this text
- Obtaining and understanding the most recent version of the *Starfish Training Center Administrative Manual*, which is available through your affiliated training center or the Starfish Aquatics Institute intranet site

Instructor Evaluations

The Course Completion Authorization form contains a section that allows your students to evaluate the quality of your instruction. Responses to questions that rate your program are monitored, and instructors who receive unfavorable ratings are contacted to begin a remediation process.

Teaching the StarGuard Course

As mentioned earlier, you may teach the StarGuard course either as a blended course, in which students first complete online courses in emergency care and lifeguarding and then experience face-to-face training, or as a series of traditional classroom and pool activities. For more information on the blended course, see chapter 4.

To run an accredited StarGuard course, you must follow the course requirements. You also must prepare properly for teaching, adhere to safety guidelines, and follow the procedures for evaluating your students and granting them certification. For those who choose to teach the waterpark, waterfront, or wilderness specialty modules, we briefly describe those requirements later in the chapter.

Course Requirements

Students in a StarGuard course must be at least 16 years old or 15 with instructor approval. The student-to-instructor ratio is a maximum of 12 students per instructor. Students must successfully complete activities for water skills screening. The screening activities confirm that a student can swim at a level appropriate for the required in-water course work. Minimum requirements include performing a 100-yard (or 100-meter) head-up swim (including 50 yards [50 meters] with a rescue tube), retrieving a submerged 10-pound (4.5-kilogram) diving brick or submersible manikin, and treading water for one minute without using the hands. You may require additional screening for your class based on your selection criteria. Some states require additional screening activities:

- Florida: Swim 200 yards (or 200 meters) of nonstop, freestyle stroke
- New York (pool module): Swim 300 yards (or 300 meters) nonstop, using various strokes in good form; surface dive to a minimum depth of 9 feet (3 meters) and bring a 10-pound (4.5-kilogram) object to the surface; tread water for one minute
- New York (waterfront module): Complete a 25-yard (or 25-meter) freestyle swim in 20 seconds; perform a shallow dive, sprint 25 yards (or 25 meters), recover a 10-pound (4.5-kilogram) nonsubmerged object from the pool edge or gutter, return 25 yards (or 25 meters), supporting the 10-pound (4.5-kilogram) object, and tread water for one minute holding a 10-pound diving brick with both hands

StarGuard lifeguard candidates must have the following textbooks: *StarGuard: Best Practices for Lifeguards* and *Essentials in Basic Emergency Care.* The text on emergency care includes the American Safety and Health Institute curriculum for bloodborne pathogens, CPR, emergency oxygen, automated external defibrillation, and basic first aid.

Instructors should be able to teach the course in 20 to 24 hours. The standard course is designed to be taught in five 4-hour modules, but instructors should spend as much time as it takes for students to meet the objectives for the course. Depending on the needs of your training center, you may also divide the modules into different lengths. For example, rather than 5 four-hour modules, you may choose to offer 10 two-hour modules.

The total number of hours to complete the blended course is also 20 to 24 hours. Face-to-face instruction should take 8 hours, and the two online courses 6 to 8 hours each.

This guide lists an average time to complete each activity. This is for your reference only to help guide the pace and flow of the course and does not dictate how much time you must spend on a particular topic. The time to complete each activity will vary according to the ability of students to learn, the number of students, and environmental considerations such as the availability of pool time and weather conditions if you are teaching outdoors. Because of the integrated nature of the curriculum, several concepts and skills (e.g., victim recognition) are taught concurrently across several activities. The training is general; therefore, the recommended minimum times to complete the objectives may not satisfy all occupational requirements specific to the unique hazards of a particular aquatic facility.

Preparation

The following are suggestions to help your training run smoothly:

- Inspect the physical environment (pool, deck, locker and rest rooms, meeting room) for safety hazards.
- Monitor the air and water temperature, and adjust it to comfortable levels.
- Ensure that pool chemicals are within acceptable ranges.
- Organize equipment and supplies.
- Set up a comfortable seating area.
- Communicate clear directions to the class regarding the location of the locker and rest rooms, pool, and staging areas for activities.

The following equipment should be available for the course:

One per Student

- Student manuals (Distribute books and assign reading before training begins.)
- Barrier mask
- Exam and answer sheet
- Course completion card and course authorization form
- Pen or pencil
- Latex or vinyl gloves (Provide several pairs per student, and be aware that some students may be allergic to latex.)
- Whistle

One per Three Students

- Rescue tube
- Manikin
- Barrier mask with plastic valve (no fiber filter) that can make a seal in the water
- Adjunct equipment (emergency oxygen, bag-valve masks, suction device, automated external defibrillator [AED] trainer)
- Bodily-fluids cleanup trainer kit (fake blood, vomit, and fecal matter; cleanup supplies; safety cones—optional; hair gel—optional)

One per Six Students

- Backboard with head immobilizer device (HID) and body straps
- Diving brick or submersible manikin
- First aid training kit or pack, including disconnected phones to practice calling 9-1-1
- Soft item that can be tossed in or out of the water (e.g., starfish bath toy, foam ball)

If you do not have enough training equipment to meet the recommended ratios, stagger their use by small groups of students while keeping other students engaged in a curriculum activity that does not require equipment. Avoid situations in which the majority of students stand around watching a few students use the equipment.

Safety

In addition to inspecting the area for safety hazards, be sure to follow these guidelines to minimize the risk of injury or illness to yourself or students during your class:

- Schedule constant and dedicated surveillance during all water activities.
- Follow manikin disinfection procedures. Clean manikins and masks after each use with a solution of 9 parts water to 1 part bleach or the manufacturer's suggested equivalent.

- Warn students not to participate in scenarios that involve extricating or moving people if they have a history of back pain or injury. An extreme or awkward body position can aggravate an injury and should be avoided.
- Warn students not to compress, ventilate, or thrust during student-on-student emergency care practice. Student-on-student practice provides necessary training for handling the human body, but the actual skills of compressions, ventilations, and removal of foreign body airway obstructions should be practiced on manikins.
- Identify and communicate to students the emergency action plan for the facility and location of the first aid kit, emergency equipment, fire and emergency exits, and evacuation routes.
- All course instructors and students should use only a feetfirst entry into the water during class sessions, regardless of water depth.
- All course instructors and students should apply sunscreen with a minimum SPF rating of 30 before outdoor class sessions.

Student Evaluation Guidelines

To successfully complete the StarGuard course, a student must pass a written or oral assessment of knowledge with a score of 80 percent; the basic StarGuard exam consists of a minimum of 40 questions, and the specialty modules for waterpark, waterfront, and wilderness include additional exam questions.

The student must also demonstrate reasonable ability to manage the following aquatic emergencies:

- Single rescuer, conscious drowning victim:
  - One-victim rescue
  - Multiple-victim rescue
- Single rescuer, unconscious drowning victim:
  - Basic life support scenario
  - Integrating adjunct equipment (if available)
- Illness and injury management
  - Spinal-injury management on land
  - Spinal-injury management in shallow water
  - Spinal-injury management in deep water
  - Control of external bleeding, care for shock
  - Manual stabilization of suspected skeletal injuries
  - Care for asthma attack, seizure, allergic reaction, and diabetic emergency
  - Care for hypothermia and hyperthermia
  - Care for a decreased level of responsiveness
  - Placement of a person in the recovery position
- Team rescue, conscious drowning victim (two-guard rescue)
- Team rescue, unconscious drowning victim:
  - Basic life support scenario, including obstructed airway management
  - Integrating adjunct equipment (if available)

Students may demonstrate competency either during a training session or in a separate evaluation session.

Certification

Upon meeting the objectives of the course, students will receive completion authorization (certification) for the following courses:

- StarGuard lifeguard
- Waterpark, waterfront, or wilderness module (if taught)
- American Safety and Health Institute (ASHI) CPR
- ASHI basic first aid
- ASHI bloodborne pathogens
- ASHI emergency oxygen
- ASHI AED training

StarGuard authorization, including the integrated ASHI courses, is valid for one year. Students must demonstrate their competency and undergo skills reevaluation annually.

The StarGuard course-completion card indicates the depth of water in which the student has demonstrated reasonable competency during training. This designation is for information purposes only; the employer must verify competency at greater depths based on site-specific circumstances. For example, if the training course was conducted in 9 feet (3 meters) of water and the facility at which the lifeguard works has water 12.5 feet (4 meters) deep, the employer should verify the competency of the lifeguard at that site-specific depth.

The Course Completion Authorization form serves as the official record of certification. This form is valid when and if the student has signed the Statement of Understanding section of the form and an authorized instructor has signed the Instructor Verification section of the form. If more than one instructor taught the course, refer to the additional instructors by their instructor number.

The carbonless Course Completion Authorization form has three copies. The Starfish Aquatics Institute national office retains one copy. The training center retains the second copy for three years or according to site-specific employment practices. The third copy is for the student (if the training center or employer has paid for the student to take the course, the authorization form may belong to the employer and might not be given directly to the student).

Renewal or Crossover Performance Challenge

Certified lifeguards may renew their StarGuard certification or cross over from another agency by either enrolling in a StarGuard course or successfully completing a challenge course on StarGuard's performance objectives. The challenge course is also available to people that have met the knowledge objectives of the StarGuard course through the blended-learning online education format and have a certificate documenting successful completion of the online training. The challenge course provides an opportunity for instructor-led skill practice, experiential scenarios, updates on new techniques or information, and evaluation of competency. The challenge course is available to candidates who meet any of the following criteria:

- Hold a current StarGuard authorization. There is a 30-day grace period after the renewal date on the authorization form during which a guard is allowed into a renewal course or crossover challenge. However, the grace period does not extend the period of authorization or certification.
- Hold an official verification certificate showing successful completion of the lifeguarding and emergency care online courses.
- Hold a current lifeguard certification, authorization, or license (or are within 30 days of expiration) from a nationally recognized agency *and* are currently employed by the authorized training center that will conduct the StarGuard course.

Specialty Modules

You may offer students one or more of five specialty modules. You may teach them concurrently with the basic StarGuard course or conduct them as separate training sessions.

Waterpark. Lifeguards who complete the waterpark module receive training in prevention, surveillance, management of conscious and unconscious victims, and professionalism and personal safety skills specific to facilities with waterslides, wave pools, water-play structures, moving water, and so on.

Average additional time when taught concurrently with StarGuard: 2 hours

Average time when taught as a separate session: 4 hours

Waterfront. Lifeguards who complete the waterfront module receive training in prevention, surveillance, management of conscious and unconscious victims, and professionalism and personal safety skills specific to nonsurf open bodies of water with restricted swim areas.

Average additional time when taught concurrently with StarGuard: 2 hours

Average time when taught as a separate session: 4 hours

Wilderness. Lifeguards and people who lead and supervise trips who complete the wilderness module receive training in prevention, surveillance, management of conscious and unconscious victims, and professionalism and personal safety skills specific to wilderness water environments, such as lakes, rivers, and streams, where access to emergency medical systems (EMS) may be more than an hour away.

Average additional time when taught concurrently with StarGuard: 10 hours

Average time when taught as a separate session: 21 hours

Emergency oxygen. Lifeguards who complete the emergency oxygen module are trained to integrate oxygen into emergency care protocols.

Average additional time when taught concurrently with StarGuard: 1 hour

Average time when taught as a separate session: 2 hours

Automated external defibrillation (AED). Lifeguards who complete the AED module are trained to integrate AED equipment into unconscious-victim protocols.

Average additional time when taught concurrently with StarGuard: 1 hour

Average time when taught as a separate session: 3 hours

Additional instructional resources for these modules are located on the Starfish Aquatics Institute intranet site. Specific information on how to obtain and use these materials will be provided during your instructor development course or through your training center.

Using the Block Plan Tool

The StarGuard block plan has been carefully crafted to provide a rewarding learning experience for students and instructors. The block plan model has been tested with hundreds of StarGuard students, reevaluated, and constantly refined—a process that will continue. However, the block plan is meant to be a tool, not a mandate. Because every training situation is different, and because each StarGuard course must meet the needs of the students, assess your needs and adapt your sessions accordingly.

Because you are unlikely to know the individual learning style of each student in your course, a variety of strategies are built into the block plan to meet the learning needs of all participants. Sessions are designed to move students through the five components of the Starfish risk management model. Often, activities are designed with an integrated, holistic approach and meet objectives across several components. For example, victim-recognition training is built into and is a part of several activities.

The block plan also considers the culture of your student audience. The following describes a majority of students in lifeguard courses:

- Between the ages of 15 and 19
- Preparing for a first job and entry into the workplace
- Enrolling in a lifeguard course for the first time
- Enrolling in a course during the school year or after the school year has ended but within days of starting a summer job

These demographics demand a training-course delivery that is concise and fast paced and challenging enough to get results.

The remaining chapters in this text provide detailed summary outlines on how to conduct a StarGuard course using the block plan. Instructor notes appear in italics or in parentheses throughout the session outlines and may include definitions, reminders, expected responses to questions, or other key points. Activity boxes provide the instructions that students may need to complete the activity and are designed to be copied, if desired, onto a flip chart, poster, or whiteboard for use during the training session.

The block plan activities should be organized differently if you are teaching a blended course or a challenge course. In appendix G is an outline that suggests how to reorganize the block plan activities when teaching such courses.

Time management will likely be one of the most challenging aspects of using the block plan to conduct a StarGuard course. You must be a skilled instructor to cover all of the content, while engaging and involving your students, in a limited time frame. Add to this challenge the logistics of moving students from meeting room, to pool, and back again, and your role as the timekeeper becomes crucial. Your students should also share this responsibility; make it clear that they must respect starting times and break times.

Facilitating Block 1

Goals	1. Gauge student experience level and swimming ability. 2. Begin team building. 3. Introduce basic life support (BLS) and bloodborne pathogens skills in order to provide a foundation for performing integrated CPR scenarios later in the course. 4. Begin to develop in students a change in attitude regarding the importance of and risks related to the job of a lifeguard.
Skill objectives	By the end of this block, students will be able to perform the following: 1. Feetfirst surface dive and retrieval of an object from the bottom 2. Approach stroke with a rescue tube 3. Bodily-substance cleanup 4. Proper removal of latex gloves 5. Emergency response sequence 6. Initial assessment of an unconscious person, including 9-1-1 call 7. Airway management according to American Heart Association (AHA) CPR/emergency cardiac care (ECC) guidelines 8. Breathing management according to AHA CPR/ECC guidelines 9. Circulation assessment according to AHA CPR/ECC guidelines.
Average time	4 hours (50 percent wet, 50 percent dry)
Overview	A. Preparing for block 1 (15 minutes) B. Water skills screening and course orientation (50 minutes) C. Bloodborne pathogens and bodily-substance isolation (60 minutes) D. Chain of survival (15 minutes) E. Airway management and rescue breathing (70 minutes) F. Who Wants to Be a Lifeguard? (20 minutes) G. Closing activity (10 minutes)
Text reference	*StarGuard: Best Practices for Lifeguards, Third Edition*, chapters 3 and 7; *Essentials in Basic Emergency Care* textbook, sections on airway management, rescue breathing, foreign body airway obstruction, and bloodborne pathogens

(continued)

(continued)

Materials (See administrative guidelines in chapter 5 for per-student ratios.)	Barrier masks
	Latex or vinyl gloves
	Rescue tubes
	Bodily-fluids cleanup trainer kit (fake blood, vomit, and fecal matter; cleanup supplies; safety cones—optional; hair gel—optional)
	Diving brick or submersible manikin
	Soft, tossable item (e.g., starfish bath toy, foam ball)
	Beach balls or similar type balls
	Have You Ever? question cards
	Hat or basket for holding cards
	Bloodborne pathogens pretest
	Pens or pencils
	Who Wants to Be a Lifeguard? questions
	Manikins (adult, child, infant)
	Study guides (online at www.starfishaquatics.webexone.com)
	Optional: two phones (for role-playing) and nonskid rubber mats

Preparing for Block 1 (15 minutes)

Step 1—Greet students and read aloud the learner skill objectives for the block. Tell students that you would like them to stand and form a circle so that everyone can get to know each other's names. Place yourself in the middle of the circle. Ideally, there should be no more than 12 students in the circle.

Step 2—Lead the group in the Have You Ever . . . ? activity. Say, "One person will be in the middle of the circle, like I am. I'm going to *loudly* and *clearly* say my name, and then I want you to do this: (demonstrate the slap, slap, clap, clap, snap, snap, shout-name sequence). Good (or repeat until students get the idea and are participating). Next, I'm going to pick a question from this (hat, bucket, bag) and read it *loudly* and *clearly.* If you can answer yes to the question, all of you, including the person who asked the question, should move off your space and then find an empty spot. It's like musical chairs; someone will always be left in the middle." Pick and read the first question to start the activity.

Sample questions for this activity are located in appendix D, or you can create your own to obtain the information you need about the experience of your students. Consider using some type of nonskid material to mark students' spots around the circle, such as thin rubber placemats cut into squares or stars. These marks help students locate vacant spots. For groups of more than six participants, consider forbidding students to move to an empty space on either side of their current location. This forces more movement through the middle of the circle as students try to find an empty spot.

Instructor outcomes: Assessment of students' experience level and ability to speak in a commanding voice

Student outcomes: Understanding that this course will be active, different, and fun; introduction to other students

Have You Ever . . . ?

1. Stand in a circle, with one person in the middle.
2. Person in the middle: *Loudly* say your name.
3. All: Slap, slap, clap, clap, snap, snap, *shout* name.
4. Person in the middle: Pull out a question and read it *loudly*.
5. All: Can you answer yes? Move to an empty spot.
6. Person left in the middle: Repeat.

Step 3—Lead the group in the Name Toss activity. Give one student a small, soft object such as a stuffed starfish, soft ball, or bean bag. Say, "I want you to *loudly* say your name, then toss the item to someone else in the circle. Remember who you throw it to and get it from. After you've received the (item), cross your arms over your chest so that others will know you're already in the pattern. Ready, begin."

Repeat the pattern two times. Then say, "This time, don't say your own name before throwing. Instead, thank the person, by name, who threw the (item) to you. For example, John is throwing to Brian. Brian catches it and says, 'Thank you, John.'" In the next round, say, "Now I want you to add, 'You're welcome' by name. For example, Brian gets the (item) from John and says, 'Thank you, John,' and John will say, 'You're welcome, Brian.'"

Instructor outcomes: Learning names and setting up for the next activity

Student outcome: Learning names

Name Toss

1. Stand in a circle.
2. Catch the item.
3. Say your name.
4. Toss the item to someone who hasn't received it.
5. Cross your arms.
6. Remember the pattern. Repeat.
7. Add "thank you" and "you're welcome" by name.

Step 4—After your students have completed a few rounds of the Name Toss activity, lead the group in the Toss Challenge activity. Say, "We will no longer say names as the item is tossed, but instead are going for time. I'll start the clock when the first toss begins and stop it when the last person receives the (item)."

After timing the first trial, say, "That was good, but you can do it faster. What is your goal time?" Let the group determine a goal time and repeat the activity, timing and repeating until they achieve the goal time. Give positive reinforcement for reaching the goal. Then say, "I'm going to give you a bigger challenge. I think you can do it in three seconds. But there are two rules: The pattern has to be completed in the same order, and everyone must touch the object. You have one minute to get ready for the challenge." Have the group attempt, evaluate strategy, and attempt again until they meet the objective.

Instructor outcomes: Identification of leaders and group dynamics

Student outcomes: Opportunity to begin developing teamwork and problem-solving skills

Water Skills Screening and Course Orientation (50 minutes)

Step 1—Direct students to the locker rooms to change and then to the staging area in the pool where you will conduct skills screening.

Step 2—Explain to students that the primary goal of the water skills screening is to determine if each person has the necessary swimming skills to safely participate in the course.

Skills Screening

1. Swim 100 yards (or 100 meters), 50 yards (or 50 meters) of it with a rescue tube.
2. Retrieve a submerged object that weighs a minimum of 10 pounds (4.5 kilograms).
3. Tread water for one minute without using the hands.

Additional local requirements: Florida—Swim 200 yards (or 200 meters) nonstop using a freestyle stroke; New York (pool module)—Swim 300 yards (or 300 meters) nonstop using various strokes in good form; surface dive to 9 feet (3 meters) and retrieve a 10-pound (4.5-kilogram) object; New York (waterfront module)—swim 25 yards (or 25 meters) using a freestyle stroke in 20 seconds; perform a shallow dive, sprint 25 yards (or 25 meters), recover a 10-pound (4.5 kilogram) nonsubmerged object from the pool edge or gutter, return 25 yards (or 25 meters), and tread water for one minute holding a 10-pound (4.5-kilogram) diving brick with both hands.

Step 3—Identify the following course safety rules and other site-specific considerations. After stating each rule, pick a student by name and ask, "Why do you think this is a course rule?"

- Use a feetfirst entry—always.

  Answer: To reduce the risk of head, neck, or spine injury

- Don't enter the water unless surveillance is in place. (Point out the lifeguard.)

  Answer: So that if an emergency occurs, a lifeguard can recognize it and respond

- Remove watches, dangling jewelry, and exposed body piercing (other than ear).

  Answer: To avoid injury to ourselves or others

- Keep the rescue tube between you and the other person.

Answer: To keep contact with flotation, to keep from being grabbed

- Apply sunscreen with a minimum SPF value of 30 (if outdoors).

  Answer: To keep from getting sunburned and reduce the risk of skin cancer

Instructor outcome: Setting of ground rules

Student outcomes: Opportunity to think about and verbalize risk management concepts

Step 4—Use a creative method to divide your class into even teams of six or fewer (see chapter 2).

Step 5—Conduct the Focus Swim Relay. Line up teams in lanes in the water (shallow, if possible). Provide each team with a light ball that floats, such as a beach ball or playground ball. Ask each team to decide the order in which its members will swim. Say, "You will each swim 50 yards (or 50 meters) freestyle while keeping the ball in front of you. You must keep the ball in sight at all times. After 50 yards (50 meters), pass the ball to the next teammate at the wall. First person: ready, go." As students swim, observe their skill level to determine if they can maintain forward progress and have the endurance to complete the distance.

At the end of the activity, ask "When and why might you need to swim using the technique you just performed?"

Answer: You would use this technique when swimming out to a person in trouble or when you need to sight the location in case he or she submerges.

Do not encourage competition between relay teams if you do not know the fitness level of the students on each team. The peer pressure of this activity can cause students to push themselves too hard and cause overexertion symptoms such as hyperventilation or vomiting, or trigger preexisting medical conditions such as asthma.

Instructor outcomes: Assessment of students' swimming ability and endurance level

Student outcomes: Opportunity to discover and practice the skill of swimming while sighting a person in need of rescue

Focus Swim Relay

1. Start in the water
2. Swim 50 yards (50 meters) freestyle.
3. Keep the ball in sight at all times.

Step 6—Conduct the Rescue Tube Relay. This relay is the same as the swim relay, except the students swim with a rescue tube. Say, "This is a rescue tube. Place the strap diagonally across your chest like this (demonstrate). Gather up the excess strap and hold it or tuck it behind the tube so that it does not get caught on anything (demonstrate). You will start in the water and swim 50 yards (50 meters), keeping the rescue tube across your chest. Use any combination of arm or leg movements that allows you to swim your fastest. There is a (identify an item to be the focal point such as starting block or poster on the wall) at the other end. This (item) represents a person in trouble in the water. Keep this focal point in your sight at all times while you are swimming with the rescue tube. First person: ready, go." The pool space and number of rescue tubes available will determine the number of teams you have and whether or not students will pass the rescue tube between team members. As students complete the activity, observe whether each person is reasonably able to maintain forward progress while swimming with the rescue tube.

Instructor outcomes: Assessment of swimming skill and endurance levels and approach stroke skill

Student outcomes: Opportunity to discover and practice the skill of swimming with a rescue tube (approach stroke)

Rescue Tube Relay

1. Start in the water.
2. Swim 50 yards (50 meters).
3. Keep the rescue tube across the chest.
4. Keep sight of the focal point at all times.

Step 7—Ask a student to demonstrate a standard surface dive and a feetfirst surface dive. Ask, "Which method of getting to the bottom do you think would be safer for you. Why?" *Answer: Feetfirst would be safer because it would be harder for someone under the water to grab your head and upper body.*

Explain that for skills-screening purposes, students can use either a standard or a feetfirst technique, but that you would like everyone to try the feetfirst technique. Point out these performance tips:

- Keep the body straight and legs tightly together.
- With your palms at your sides, turn them up toward the surface.
- Push the water toward the surface by quickly lifting your arms toward the surface. Your body will go down as you push up.
- Slide your arms down the front of your body back into position at your side. Repeat the push toward the surface as needed to submerge to the desired depth.

Step 8—Conduct the Retrieval Relay. Team members are all in the water, with one rescue tube per team. Each team member holds onto the tube with one hand. Submerge a weighted object, such as a diving brick. The first team member performs a feetfirst surface dive to retrieve the object and bring it to the surface. He or she then replaces the object on the bottom, and the next student dives to retrieve the object. To avoid dropping weighted objects to the pool floor, require that the object be swum back to the bottom as part of the relay. If you have several diving bricks or objects, teams can compete against each other at the same time. An alternative is to time each team to determine a winner.

Instructor outcomes: Assessment of ability to retrieve an object from the bottom and make a feetfirst surface dive

Student outcomes: Ability to perform a feetfirst surface dive and retrieve an object

Retrieval Relay

1. Each member of the group holds onto the rescue tube.
2. One member does a feetfirst surface dive, picks up an object from the bottom of the pool, returns to the surface, then returns the object to the bottom.
3. The next person performs the exercise.
4. Team members perform the exercise until everyone has had a turn.

Step 9—Students form a circle in the water and perform the Name Toss Tread. The activity is the same as the Name Toss activity that you performed on land, but is conducted while students tread water. Students should keep their hands above the surface to catch the item and place their arms across their chest when they have received and thrown the item.

Instructor outcome: Assessment of students' ability to tread water

Student outcomes: Reinforcement of names; development of camaraderie and confidence; opportunity to practice treading water

Step 10—Congratulate students on completing the skills screening and being eligible to continue in the course.

Step 11—Distribute barrier masks, gloves, and other training equipment and books if your students have not received them in advance.

Step 12—Review the start times of each session and other course-specific announcements. Distribute the study guide (if students have not received this in advance) and explain that the study guide must be completed before taking the written exam. You can obtain the study guide master for duplicating from the password-protected instructor area on the Starfish Aquatics Institute's intranet site.

Bloodborne Pathogens and Bodily-Substance Isolation (60 minutes)

Step 1—Pose the question, "Why do you think we are starting the course with the topic of bloodborne pathogens and bodily-substance isolation?" *Answer: Because our personal protection and safety is a top priority.*

Step 2—Identify the tie-in to real experience. Say, "When we did the Have You Ever . . . ? activity, you remember that there were several questions such as 'Have you ever cleaned up vomit, blood, or feces from a pool?' All of you who have been lifeguards before moved on that question. Tell us about your experience."

Step 3—Have students complete the bloodborne pathogens pretest. If the pretest is not available in the student manual, a master for duplication is available in the password-protected instructor area on the Starfish Aquatics Institute intranet site. When finished, have students break into small groups and agree on the answer to each question, using the bloodborne pathogens sections of the student manuals as a reference. Monitor discussions to identify which questions needed further clarification.

Instructor outcomes: Assessment of knowledge and student needs

Student outcomes: Reinforcement or development of understanding of blood-borne pathogen concepts

Step 4—Conduct a discussion that includes the following:

- Review, with the entire group, of topics that need further clarification
- Recreational water illness (caused by E. coli, giardia, cryptosporidium) and the need for specialized cleanup procedures at aquatic facilities, a swim diaper policy, and patron education
- Your local health department regulations regarding fecal incidents in the water

Step 5—Demonstrate your site-specific procedure for cleaning up bodily substances on the pool deck or locker room and pool area floor.

Step 6—Conduct the Blood, Feces, Vomit activity. Divide students into groups and conduct scenarios for the following:

- Blood on the deck
- Vomit on the deck
- Fecal matter on the deck

Fake blood, vomit, and feces (including fake dirty diapers) can be obtained from costume and novelty stores. Do not use real bleach during practice; instead, use water in containers marked "simulated bleach." To avoid the expense of using commercial bodily-fluids cleanup kits during training, make your own packs of absorbing material by placing a small amount of kitty litter in snack-size plastic bags. If you do not have preprinted biohazard disposal bags, use a garbage bag with a biohazard sticker. Small orange safety cones are ideal for marking the area and simulating access restriction.

Blood, Feces, Vomit

1. Contain—secure area.
2. Personal protection equipment—put on gloves.
3. Remove—wipe up, using absorbing material if available.
4. Disinfect—soak area with bleach solution for five minutes.
5. Dispose—place material into bags marked with the biohazard symbol.
6. Restrict use of area—follow local health department guidelines.

Step 7—Demonstrate the proper method for removing gloves to avoid exposure to bodily substances.

Step 8—Ask students to put on gloves, then squirt hair gel into the palms of their hands, stating that the substance is contaminated. Have the students remove their gloves and dispose of them in a biohazard bag. Then ask, "Do any of you have sticky spots on your hands or arms? If so, you have been 'exposed' to a contaminated bodily substance. What should you do?"

Answer: We should wash exposed areas and hands, report the incident to the supervisor, and get medical attention as directed.

Instructor outcome: Assessment of students' understanding of bloodborne pathogens

Student outcomes: Ability to perform bodily substance cleanup and glove removal; knowledge of what to do if contaminated

Chain of Survival (15 minutes)

Step 1—Ask, "Who knows what EMS stands for?" *Answer: It stands for emergency medical system.* Ask, "What does that mean?" Discuss and wrap up with the EMS definition. *Answer: EMS is a network of resources—people, communications, and equipment—organized to provide emergency care to victims of sudden illness or injury.*

Step 2—Ask, "Where do lifeguards fit into this system?" *Answer: We call EMS as early in an emergency as possible, then provide care until they arrive.*

Step 3—Explain that the first person to respond to the scene must follow three initial steps during an emergency: Assess, alert, and attend. Ask, "What does 'assess' mean?" *Answer: It means to look at what is happening and decide to take action based on what is found.* Ask, "What two things must you assess during an emergency?" *Answer: Is the scene safe? Is the person O.K.? Explain that another word for "assess" is "survey," which means "to look."* Ask, "What are you looking for when you survey the scene?" *Answer: We're looking for obvious hazards such as downed wires, fallen objects, wildlife, chemicals (and so on); clues to what may have happened; and for others involved.* Ask, "What else has to happen at the scene for you to be safe before you touch the person?" *Answer: We have to put on gloves.*

Step 4—Ask, "Now that we've assessed the scene, we have to assess the condition of the person. How can you do that?" *Answer: You can do that by going up to the person.* Next, explain what to do in the following situations: If the person is conscious, the lifeguard should tell the person his or her name, that he or she knows first aid, and ask for permission to help. If the person gives permission, the lifeguard should continue with the assessment and decide whether or not to take action, possibly calling 9-1-1. If the person denies permission, the lifeguard should move away from the situation and contact a supervisor. If the person is unresponsive, the lifeguard should put on gloves, shake the person, and shout, "Are you O.K.? Are you O.K.?"

Step 5—Explain that if the person remains unresponsive, the next step is to alert someone that he or she needs help by yelling for help, or if someone is near, directing him or her to call 9-1-1 and come back to the scene. The idea is to "phone first and phone fast" to get EMS on the way as quickly as possible. Explain that in situations where a rescuer is by himself or herself, the decision to leave the unresponsive person to call 9-1-1 and obtain an AED (if available) should be based on the likely cause of unresponsiveness. If an adult has suddenly collapsed, the likely cause is a heart attack and the lone rescuer should phone first, obtain the AED, then return to start CPR. In all instances of submersion, the lone rescuer should begin CPR first and provide about 5 cycles (or about 2 minutes) of CPR before leaving to call 9-1-1 and obtain the AED. In all instances of unconsciousness in infants or children, regardless of the likely cause, this CPR-first sequence should also be followed.

Step 6—Conduct the 9-1-1 Call activity. One student role-plays calling 9-1-1, and another student role-plays receiving the call as a dispatcher. Disconnected phones can be used as props for this activity.

Calling 9-1-1 Script

Dispatcher: 9-1-1. This call is recorded. What is the nature of your emergency?

Caller: A woman is unconscious at the county's Longwood Pool.

Dispatcher: Is your location 7420 Long Drive?

Caller: No, that's another county building. We're at 1540 Wood Street. Please hurry.

Dispatcher: O.K. Help is being sent even while you're talking to me. When did this happen?

Caller: I think the lifeguards have been doing CPR for a couple of minutes already.

Dispatcher: What is your name?

Caller: Chris Fuller.

Dispatcher: What is the phone number you are calling from?

Caller: 555-2432

Dispatcher: Do you know the approximate age of the person?

Caller: I think the lady is Mrs. Smith. She's middle aged.

Dispatcher: Was she in the water when she went unconscious?

Caller: I don't know; I was just told to call 9-1-1. I work at the check-in desk at the front.

Dispatcher: O.K. The medical unit should arrive soon.

Caller: Yes, I hear the sirens.

Dispatcher: You can hang up and direct them to the scene.

Step 7—Debrief the activity. Ask, "What were the top priorities of the EMS dispatcher?" *Answer: The priorities were to calm the caller, keep the caller on the line, collect information (where, what, when, who, why), and provide prearrival instructions.* Ask, "Why didn't the correct address come up on the dispatcher's screen?" *Answer: The phone at the pool was on a countywide networked system that rotates through numbers assigned to different locations. That's why it's important to have the address posted near each phone.* Ask, "How would this call have been different if the caller had been panicked?" *Answers: It would have taken longer. Assumptions might have led to giving incorrect information, such as "a lady drowned."*

Step 8—Demonstrate the steps of emergency response: Assess the scene and the person's condition, alert, and attend.

Step 9—Divide students into pairs to practice the steps of emergency response. One person should be in need of assistance, and the other should be the responder.

Airway Management and Rescue Breathing (Average time: 70 minutes)

Step 1—Ask, "What is your airway?" *Answer: The airway is the part of your body that carries air from your nose and mouth to your lungs. It is also called the trachea.*" Ask, "What happens if a person's airway is blocked?" *Answer: A person with a blocked airway has no chance of survival because oxygen cannot get to the brain. This is why opening the airway and ventilating the person with two initial rescue breaths are the first priority of care.* Ask, "What causes a person's airway to become blocked?" *Answer: A person swallows something that gets stuck in the airway and blocks it; this is also called choking. Also, an unconscious person loses muscle tone, which may allow the soft tissue and base of the tongue to block the airway, or the airway may be filled with water or vomit.*

Step 2—Demonstrate opening the airway for an adult or child using the head-tilt, chin-lift method. Debrief the activity. Ask, "Why did I tilt the head backward?" *Answer: This straightens the airway.* Use an analogy of a kinked water hose. Until the hose is straightened, water cannot get through. Ask, "Why did I lift the chin?" *Answer: Because the tongue is attached to the lower jaw, moving the jaw forward lifts the tongue away from the back of the throat.*

Point out these performance tips:

- Sometimes opening an airway is all that is needed to restore spontaneous breathing.
- Do not press into the soft tissues of the chin.
- Do not use the thumb to lift the chin.
- The mouth must be open—look in the mouth for fluids, solids, teeth, and dentures.
- If you suspect that the person has a head, neck, or back injury, use the chin-lift method without the head tilt. This is sometimes called a jaw-thrust maneuver. If you are not able to effectively open the airway with this maneuver, use the head-tilt, chin-lift method, since opening the airway is a priority for the unconscious person.

Step 3—Demonstrate opening the airway for an infant using a head-neutral, chin lift. Debrief the activity. Ask, "What did I do differently for the infant?" *Answer: You tilted the head only a very small amount.* Explain that an infant's airway is different from that of someone older. Use the analogy of the water hose—if it is folded either forward, or backward, no water can get through. This is similar to what can happen to an infant's airway if the head is tilted too far back.

Step 4—Demonstrate opening the airway for an adult or child using the triple airway maneuver. Debrief the activity. Point out these performance tips:

- Position yourself behind the person's head.
- Pick up the head slightly before tilting it back.

- This technique allows for maximum airway control and is usually used when there are two rescuers—one to manage the airway and the other to provide compressions if the person does not have a pulse.
- This technique allows more room to accommodate other rescuers and adjunct equipment next to the person.

Step 5—Divide the group into pairs to practice the head-tilt, chin-lift method, the triple airway maneuver for an adult, and the head-neutral, chin lift for an infant.

Step 6—Demonstrate how to check for adequate breathing in adults and the presence or absence of breathing in children and infants: look, listen, and feel for 3 to 5 seconds. Debrief the activity. Ask, "What am I looking for?" *Answer: In adults, you're looking for the even rise and fall of the chest, which is a sign of normal breathing.* Ask, "What am I listening for?" *Answer: You're listening for sounds of regular, rhythmic, breathing.* Ask, "What am I feeling for?" *Answer: You're feeling for breath coming from the mouth or nose.* Reinforce not to wait to give adults rescue breaths until all breathing stops, because adults in cardiac arrest may make gasping sounds. Unless the adult's breathing sounds normal and adequate, two initial rescue breaths should be provided to start the CPR sequence. Reinforce that for children, begin rescue breaths only if there is an absence of any breath sounds or breathing pattern.

Step 7—Conduct activities to introduce the next steps of emergency response and basic life support, including rescue breathing without chest compressions and foreign body airway obstruction. You can find suggested activities in your instructor guide for *Essentials in Basic Emergency Care* or from the password-protected instructor area on the Starfish Aquatics Institute's intranet site. These activities provide instruction based on the 2005 American Heart Association Guidelines for Cardiopulmonary Resuscitation and Emergency Cardiovascular Care.

Who Wants to Be a Lifeguard? (20 minutes)

Step 1—Divide the group into pairs so that they can interview each other using the Who Wants to Be a Lifeguard? questions. Discuss with your students what they have experienced in the first class session and how it relates to the job of a lifeguard.

Step 2—Reconvene for a presentation of the findings. Debrief by asking each partner group to describe their answers to one question. Lead brief discussion as issues arise.

Step 3—Say, "I'm going to try to summarize why we do what we do." Read the starfish story in chapter 1 of the student text. Emphasize that lifeguarding is one of the most important and rewarding jobs your students could have.

Instructor outcome: Assessment of students' attitudes toward lifeguarding

Student outcomes: Examination of motivation and attitudes toward lifeguarding; interaction with another student

Interview Questions: Who Wants to Be a Lifeguard?

1. Describe the worst lifeguarding you've ever seen. Why do you consider it the worst?
2. Describe the best lifeguarding you've ever seen. Why do you consider it the best?
3. What motivated you to become a lifeguard?
4. Have we done things in class so far that you never expected to have to do while lifeguarding?
5. What do you think most people's image of a lifeguard is? What should it be?
6. What do you think will be your biggest challenge?

Closing Activity (10 minutes)

Step 1—Conduct the I Now Know That . . . activity. Say, "I want you to reflect on the course so far and think of something that you've learned or have been reminded of. It can be anything, small or large, but I want you to phrase it by saying 'I now know that . . .' For example: I now know that swimming with a rescue tube is easier than I thought, or I now know that the rescue breathing rate for a child is one breath every 3 seconds. Keep your statement short and concise."

Step 2—Ask students to form a tight circle. Identify who will start and in which direction the responses should go. For example, say, "We will start with Jim and go to his left. Don't repeat something that someone else has already said."

Step 3—Provide instructions or reminders about the next session. Assign students to read or review the basic first aid sections of the student texts and to work on completing the study guide.

Instructor outcome: Assessment of students' experiences so far

Student outcomes: Opportunity to review, reinforce, and reflect; transition to break

Facilitating Block 2

Goals	1. Define risk management and prevention strategies. 2. Begin victim-recognition training (VRT). 3. Provide practical scanning and surveillance experience. 4. Develop conscious-victim rescue skills.
Skill objectives	By the end of this block, students will be able to perform the following: 1. Victim simulation 2. Scanning patterns and three-dimensional triage scanning 3. Ten-second scan and 5-Minute Scanning Strategy 4. Proactive rotation 5. Whistle blast 6. Compact jump 7. Front rescue 8. Rear rescue 9. Two-guard rescue 10. Leg-wrap rescue: standard and extended 11. Multiple-victim rescue 12. Emergency escape
Average time	4 hours (75 percent wet, 25 percent dry)
Overview	A. Preparing for block 2 (10 minutes) B. Starfish risk management model (15 minutes) C. Prevention assessment (30 minutes) D. Victim-recognition training (90 minutes) E. Aquatic rescue—STAAR, compact jump, escape (30 minutes) F. Aquatic rescue—front, rear, two guard (30 minutes) G. Aquatic rescue—leg wrap, multiple victim (30 minutes) H. Closing activity (5 minutes)
Text reference	*StarGuard: Best Practices for Lifeguards, Third Edition*, chapters 1, 2, 4, 5, 6, and 9
Materials *(See administrative guidelines in chapter 5 for per-student ratios.)*	Pens or pencils and paper Rescue tubes Submersible manikins, shadow dolls, or other victim-simulation items Whistles Symptom cards Closing statement cards

Preparing for Block 2 (10 minutes)

Step 1—Greet students and read aloud the learner skill objectives for the block. Tell students that staying on target and within the time limits for each activity are necessary for meeting all the objectives before the end of the session.

Starfish Risk Management Model (15 minutes)

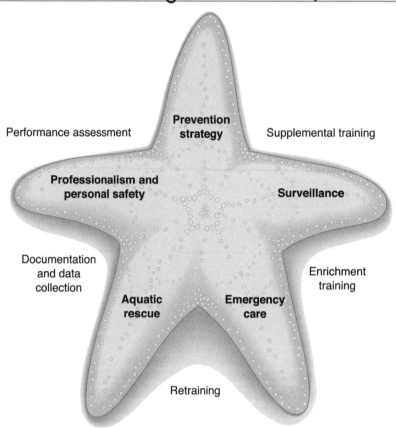

Step 1—Ask your students to draw a large starfish on a piece of paper. Ask them to write the words "risk management" in the center and the following words, one in each appendage: prevention strategy, surveillance, emergency care, aquatic rescue, professionalism and personal safety.

Step 2—Debrief the activity. Ask, "What does 'risk management' mean?" *Answer: It is all of the things in place to reduce the chance that someone will get hurt, sick, or drown.* Say, "A starfish makes a great model for these concepts because all of the parts are independent, but connected at the center. Each appendage is just as important as the others. What would happen if one of the starfish's legs were cut off? For example, what if no prevention strategies were in place at your pool?" *Answer: Chaos, injury, drowning, and so on could occur.* Ask, "What if everything else were in place, but there was no surveillance?" *Answer: A drowning would not be noticed in time to make a difference.* Ask, "What if everything else were in place, but lifeguards did not know how to provide emergency care, such as first aid and CPR?" *Answer: Sick or injured people would have to wait until EMS arrived, which could cause consequences that might have been avoided if immediate care had been given on site.* Ask, "What if the lifeguards had no aquatic rescue skills?" *Answer:*

Situations that should be easy to handle in the water might turn into drownings of the victim or of both the victim and the lifeguard. Ask, "What if lifeguards were smoking, eating, cussing, running around and throwing kids in the pool, sleeping, yelling, making out, reading, or talking on a cell phone? How would that affect risk management?" *Answer: These behaviors don't inspire respect for lifeguards, which could tempt some patrons to break the rules. These lifeguards set a bad example and don't show that they understand the risks inherent in water activities, which could keep others from taking these risks seriously. These behaviors often are a symptom that other things are wrong as well.* Ask, "What about personal safety? What would happen if a lifeguard didn't drink water throughout the day and became dehydrated?" *Answer: The lifeguard would be too sick to be vigilant and too weak to make a rescue, and he or she would look tired and inattentive.*

Alternative activity: Cut out a large cardboard starfish and write one core skill on each leg and "aquatic risk management" in the middle. Cut the starfish into five pieces and ask the class to assemble the puzzle. Then debrief as described above.

Instructor outcome: Assessment of students' understanding of risk management

Student outcome: Practical understanding of aquatic risk management

Prevention Assessment (30 minutes)

Step 1—Conduct the Walk-About activity. Tell students that they need something like a clipboard to write on, a blank sheet of paper, and something to write with. Ask them to walk about the facility for 10 minutes, identifying and listing everything that is in place to *prevent* injury or death. Examples would be specific policies or procedures, equipment, and design features of the facility. This activity may be performed individually or in groups of no more than three students.

Step 2—Reconvene to debrief the activity. Ask each student to describe an item on his or her list and briefly state the item's role in prevention.

Step 3—If someone mentions clear water as a prevention strategy, say, "Clear water is one of the most important prevention features. Why?" *Answer: Lifeguards must be able to see under the surface all the way to the bottom to be able to detect a drowning victim. Clear water is a good indication (but not 100 percent) that the disinfectant level of the water is being maintained.* If no one identifies clear water, say, "All of you missed one of the most important prevention features of this facility. What is it?" When clear water is identified, discuss as described previously.

Instructor outcomes: Assessment of students' ability to perceive prevention strategies and identify what should be in place

Student outcomes: Ability to think critically about the prevention and preparation for conducting a hazard inspection

Walk About

Walk about the facility for 10 minutes.
Write down everything in place to prevent injury, illness, and death.

Victim-Recognition Training (90 minutes)

Step 1—Conduct the Where's Timmy? activity (approximately 10 minutes). Ask students to leave the pool area. Submerge manikins, shadow dolls, or other items to represent drowning victims. Bring your students back into the area, stopping at various locations around the pool to check their ability to see the submerged objects.

Step 2—Debrief the activity. Emphasize how water can hide a submerged body and how glare, corners, walls, and raised decking can create blind spots.

- Discuss the meaning of the term *triage:* Providing care to the most critical need first.
- Discuss the concept of three-dimensional triage scanning: Scanning the bottom first because that is where someone who most critically needs care may be located.

Instructor outcome: Assessment of students' ability to identify submerged simulated drowning victims

Student outcomes: Experience in seeing what something on the pool bottom may look like and how glare and surface movement can change the ability to see below the surface; awareness of blind spots

Step 3—Conduct the zone-validation activity (approximately 10 minutes). Explain that a zone is the area a lifeguard is responsible for and must scan. Tell the students that the whole pool is their zone. Ask students to find a location for the lifeguard stand from which the entire bottom can be scanned and all of the submerged "bodies" can be seen. *In most cases, there will not be one spot from which all submerged items can be seen during a scan.* Pose the question, "The entire bottom must be scanned, and you are the only lifeguard on duty. How will you accomplish this?" *Answers (depending on the pool): The lifeguard could rove, close part of the pool, or stand on a tower. It can't be done—the area must be divided into zones and covered by additional lifeguards.*

Instructor outcome: Assessment of students' understanding of the concept of zone coverage

Student outcome: Ability to think critically about zone size and zone coverage

Step 4—Conduct the Starfish Scanning System activity (approximately 15 minutes). Ask students to draw a large starfish on a piece of paper. Ask them to write the words "scanning strategy" in the center and the following words, one in each appendage: why? where? when? how? hand-off?

Step 5—Ask, "Why should we have a scanning system?" *Answer: A scanning system allows us to recognize someone in trouble early—the earlier the intervention, the better chance for success. And it counteracts the RID (recognition, intrusion, distraction) factor.* Tell your students to write "RID factor" in the "why?" appendage of the starfish.

Step 6—Ask, "Where should we scan?" *Answer: We should scan three dimensionally, starting with the bottom first—three-dimensional triage scanning.* Tell your students to write "three-dimensional triage" in the "where?" appendage of the starfish.

Step 7—Ask, "When should we scan?" *Answer: Lifeguards should perform a three-dimensional triage scan of the zone every 10 seconds. The zone should not be so large that a lifeguard cannot scan it in 10 seconds or reach the farthest area of the zone in 20 seconds.* Tell students to write "10/20 rule" in the "when?" appendage of the starfish.

Step 8—Ask, "How should we scan?" *Answer: We should use a scanning pattern and change the pattern as well as posture (sit, stand, stroll) and position often—about every five minutes. This is the 5-Minute Scanning Strategy.* Discuss how this scanning technique, developed by Tom Griffiths, helps lifeguards remain vigilant and alert. *Some form of physical movement should occur every five minutes, as well as some form of mental activity such as counting patrons or mentally rehearsing a rescue.* Tell students to write "five-minute scan" in the "how?" appendage of the starfish.

Step 9—Ask, "When you rotate lifeguard positions and take over someone else's zone, what should you know about that zone? *Answer: You should know if the outgoing lifeguard has concerns or information about what has been happening in the zone.* Say, "That is information you need, but what if that lifeguard did not see someone slip beneath the surface and did not see the submerged person on his or her three-dimensional triage scan. Whose responsibility will the person on the bottom become?" *Answer: It becomes the incoming lifeguard's responsibility.* Say, "It is important for you to do a three-dimensional triage scan *before* you take over the zone to make sure it's clear and you're not taking over something the previous lifeguard missed. Scanning before the hand-off, as well as mentally preparing yourself to take over the zone, is called a proactive rotation." Tell your students to write "proactive rotation" in the "hand-off?" appendage of the starfish.

Starfish Scanning System

Why? RID factor
Where? Three-dimensional triage scanning
When? 10/20 rule
How? 5-Minute Scanning Strategy
Hand-off? Proactive rotation

Instructor outcome: Assessment of students' understanding of the Starfish scanning system

Student outcome: Integration of the various scanning methods into one easy-to-understand system

Step 10—Conduct the Three-Dimensional Triage activity (approximately 10 minutes) to practice scanning patterns and three-dimensional triage scanning. After students are positioned around the pool, say, "Scan your zone using a side-to-side pattern with your eyes. Use the three-dimensional triage technique as you move your eyes from side to side. I should be able to see your head move and count no more than 10 seconds before I see you begin a second sweep." Continue this pattern for at least two minutes. Say, "Now switch to an up-and-down pattern. Even though you are moving your eyes up and down, I should still be able to see your head move and count no more than 10 seconds before I see you begin a second sweep." Continue this pattern for at least two minutes. Say, "Now switch to a figure-eight pattern with your eyes." At various times during this group exercise ask, "What are you looking for?" *Answers: We're looking for lack of movement, suspicious shadows, patrons with distress symptoms, rule-breaking behavior, and so on.*

Step 11—Demonstrate a proactive rotation (approximately 10 minutes) first with a rescue tube for each lifeguard and then with two lifeguards transferring one rescue tube between them. Debrief the activity. Point out these performance tips:

- If you are a lifeguard coming in after a break, walk around the pool or zone to get to the stand if possible. What might this accomplish? *Answer: You would prepare mentally and be able to proactively scan a larger area, look for hazards, and see what's going on in the zone.*

- Exaggerate the proactive bottom scan—make it obvious what you are doing. Why? *Answer: This increases the lifeguard's visibility to the patrons and increases professionalism.*

- Say aloud, "I've got the zone" each time you take responsibility during a hand-off. Why? *Answer: This ensures that there isn't confusion about who has the zone.*

- Provide zone-related information to the incoming lifeguard if needed. Why? *Answer: This is done to make the incoming lifeguard aware of possible problems.*

Step 12—Conduct the STAAR activity (approximately 15 minutes). Ask students to draw a large starfish on a piece of paper and write the words "aquatic rescue" in the center and the following words, one in each appendage: scan, target, assess, alert, and rescue, which spell out STAAR.

Remind students of the assess, alert, and attend steps of emergency response. Explain that the same principles apply to aquatic rescue, with a few modifications. Say, "Lifeguards have the responsibility to scan before being able to assess and alert, so two steps must be added: scan and target. "Ask, "What does 'target' mean?" *Answer: It means focusing on and looking more closely at something or someone.* Ask, "What will you assess after you target something?" *Answer: We'll assess the situation to decide if that person is in trouble and if we need to take action.* Remind students of the alert step that they practiced for emergencies on land. Explain that lifeguards must have a signal to alert others that someone is in trouble and a rescue is taking place and that the signal most commonly used is a whistle or horn blast while a lifeguard stands and points to the person in trouble. Remind students that signals may differ from facility to facility. A facility's emergency action plan will describe the specific signal to be used.

Ask, "Why is a signal needed instead of just yelling for help and telling someone to call 9-1-1?" *Answers: A signal can overcome the noise around the pool and alert many people, such as other lifeguards to cover the zone, the manager, and other lifeguards to respond to help. It's not known yet if someone needs to call 9-1-1.* Explain that after alerting others, a lifeguard attends to a person by making a rescue. Ask students to stand and yell out the STAAR aquatic–rescue sequence.

Scan (three-dimensional triage)

Target (focus)

Assess (decide to take action)

Alert (whistle and point)

Rescue

Step 13—Conduct the Victim School activity (approximately 20 minutes). Assign each student a number and a symptom from table 5.1 in the student text. Each student should have a whistle.

Ask students to consider what it would be like to experience the symptom he or she has been assigned. Stress that when simulating the symptom, body position, facial expression, speed of movement, and so on should be as realistic as possible. Remind students that most victims do not splash and thrash, but exhibit subtle symptoms such as a change in movement or lack of movement.

Identify the zone and place a chair in a position from which the entire zone can be seen or use an existing lifeguard stand if available. Provide the following directions for the activity:

- One person is the "lifeguard" and all others are "patrons."
- Patrons swim and have a good time, but must follow all pool rules.
- When a patron's number is displayed (hand signals or card), he or she should exhibit the assigned symptom. When the lifeguard recognizes the behavior, he or she should stand, whistle, and point to the area.
- The student who was the victim then performs a proactive rotation into the lifeguard position.

Direct student number one to take a position in the chair. Point out proper rescue-ready posture to the students. This includes the following:

- Rescue tube worn or placed across the lap
- Strap gathered
- Feet flat on the ground or lifeguard stand platform.
- Shoulders forward

Direct other students to enter the water. Stand behind the lifeguard to coach three-dimensional triage scanning and to randomly signal the symptom numbers for the patrons. After every student has been both a patron and a lifeguard, debrief the activity. Elicit feedback from your students about what they experienced.

The following variations can enhance this activity:

- Lifeguards wear goggles or glasses that restrict peripheral vision. These devices force an exaggerated head turn and let lifeguards experience how much they rely on unrestricted sight to adequately scan.
- If you have a submersible manikin, have the student assigned to exhibit unconscious-victim symptoms take the manikin into the water with him or her without the lifeguard seeing it and drop it to the bottom when it is his or her turn.

- Display several numbers at a time to simulate multiple situations happening at once.

Instructor outcomes: Assessment of students' ability to perform scanning, proactive rotation, and victim recognition

Student outcomes: Practical experience in scanning, rotating, and recognizing distress and drowning symptoms

Aquatic Rescue—STAAR, Compact Jump, Escape (30 minutes)

Step 1—Remind students of the importance of the rescue tube and of keeping the rescue tube between themselves and a victim at all times. Identify a safety signal, such as two taps, to use during rescue practice to indicate "let go" or "stop."

Step 2—Discuss situations in which a rescuer might temporarily lose contact with a rescue tube and be grabbed by a struggling person. Ask, "What is that person's top priority?" *Answer: The rescuer must stay on the surface so that he or she can breathe.* Ask, "Knowing that, what could you do if you are grabbed that might cause the person to let go?" *Answer: You could submerge.* Ask, "If the person doesn't let go, what will you have to do?" *Answer: You must escape from his or her grasp.*

Step 3—Demonstrate an emergency escape on land and in the water. Debrief the demonstration and emphasize these performance tips:

- The first step in an escape should be to submerge—a victim wants to remain on the surface and will likely release his or her grasp on a rescuer.
- Follow the steps of suck, tuck, and duck: suck in a breath, tuck your chin, and duck out of the victim's grasp.
- Gain control of the rescue tube and try the rescue again or signal for help.

Step 4—Divide students into groups for drill practice. The size of the group depends on the number of students and pool space available. Remind students of the signal to use during water practice to indicate "let go" and "stop."

Step 5—Have students practice the emergency escape in the water.

Step 6—Demonstrate the STAAR verbal command followed by a compact jump on land and in the water. Debrief the activity and emphasize these performance tips:

- Keep the rescue tube strap gathered.
- Squeeze the rescue tube into the chest.
- A compact jump is like a "cannonball" with feet flexed.
- The body will submerge briefly, then pop to the surface. Sight the distressed swimmer or drowning victim.
- Keeping the feet flexed during a compact jump helps protect from injury if the water is shallow.

Step 7—Conduct a drill to allow students to practice compact jumps from the side. If available, and when students have performed well off the side, move to a platform, such as a starting block or lifeguard stand, for additional practice.

Instructor outcomes: Assessment of students' ability to perform a compact jump and an escape

Student outcomes: Integration of the STAAR rescue model into practical experience; performance of a compact jump and an escape

Aquatic Rescue—Front, Rear, Two Guard (30 minutes)

Step 1—Demonstrate the STAAR verbal command, followed by a compact jump, approach stroke, and front rescue on land and in the water. Debrief the demonstration and emphasize these performance tips:

- Keep the rescue tube strap gathered before the compact jump.
- Sight the distressed swimmer or drowning victim.
- Use any combination of leg kicks and arm pulls that gets you to the person the quickest.
- Push the rescue tube into the person's chest.
- Keep the arms straight once contact is made.
- Let the victim grab the tube; there is no need for the rescuer to grab the victim.

Step 2—Conduct a drill to allow students to practice the STAAR verbal command, compact jump, and front-rescue sequence. State that these drills will be for rescuing conscious people. Remind students to exhibit realistic distressed-swimmer and drowning-victim symptoms. These include the following:

- Head is back.
- Person is not kicking.
- Person is using ineffective, small, back-and-forth arm movements.
- Mouth and nose are just above the surface for a distressed swimmer or just below the surface for a drowning victim.

Step 3—Demonstrate a rear rescue on land and in the water. Debrief the demonstration and emphasize these performance tips:

- Turn your head before making contact to prevent the victim from hitting you in the face with his or her head.
- Keep the tube across your chest and reach around the person under the arms.

Step 4—Conduct a drill to allow students to practice the STAAR verbal command, compact jump, and rear-rescue sequence.

Step 5—Demonstrate the two-guard rescue on land and in the water. Debrief the demonstration and emphasize these performance tips:

- The two-guard rescue is a front rescue and rear rescue performed simultaneously.

- The initial rescuer backs away and signals for help with a raised clenched fist. He or she waits to reposition until the backup rescuer arrives.
- The rescuer behind the victim initiates the rescue in order to serve as a target for the front rescuer.

Step 6—Conduct a drill to allow students to practice the STAAR verbal command, compact jump, and two guard–rescue sequence.

> *Instructor outcomes:* Assessment of students' ability to perform a front rescue, rear rescue, and two-guard rescue
>
> *Student outcomes:* Integration of the STAAR rescue model into practical experience; performance of a front rescue, rear rescue, and two-guard rescue

Aquatic Rescue—Leg Wrap, Multiple Victim (30 minutes)

Step 1—Demonstrate the STAAR rescue components, compact jump, approach stroke, and the standard leg-wrap rescue for a submerged victim on land and in the water. Debrief the demonstration and emphasize these performance tips:

- This technique eliminates upper-body contact between the rescuer and victim.
- This technique allows the rescuer to maintain hands-on control of the rescue tube.

Step 2—Conduct a drill to allow students to practice the STAAR verbal command, compact jump, approach stroke, and leg wrap–rescue sequence.

If your students are reasonably competent in executing the STAAR rescue components, compact jump, and approach stroke, present the remaining skills from in the water to reduce the amount of time spent swimming back to the wall, climbing out, and reentering after each practice drill.

Step 3—Demonstrate the extended leg-wrap rescue on land (if practical) and in the water. Debrief the demonstration and emphasize these performance tips:

- Pull on the tube strap to raise both rescuer and victim to the surface; there is no need to swim up.
- Place the rescue tube across the chest before lifting the victim the final few feet to the surface.

Step 4—Conduct a drill to allow students to practice the STAAR verbal command, compact jump, approach stroke, and leg wrap–rescue sequence.

Step 5—Reconvene students to the deck. Elicit feedback about their experience with the various aquatic rescue techniques. Ask, "You've performed the leg-wrap technique in (indicate depth) feet of water. How would it work if the water was very deep, for example in a diving well of 16 feet (4.9 meters)?" Discuss the options presented, then demonstrate the potential depth to which the leg wrap could be extended by removing the chest strap, holding onto the end of the chest strap loop, and making a full-body extension to contact the submerged victim.

Instructor outcome: Assessment of the students' ability to perform a leg-wrap rescue

Student outcomes: Integration of the STAAR rescue model into practical experience; performance of a rescue of a submerged drowning victim using the leg-wrap technique

Step 6—Conduct the Three's a Crowd activity. Divide students into groups of four. Review the "Help, I need backup" communication signal (a raised fist) and the "let go" or "stop" signal (two taps). Remind students of the objectives of a successful rescue:

- Minimize body-to-body contact
- Keep the heads of both the rescuer and victim out of the water so they can breathe
- Progress to a takeout point

Explain that this is a problem-solving exercise, and there is no one right way to achieve the objectives. Set up two stations and rotate groups through them.

Station 1: One rescuer and three conscious drowning victims. Scenario: Two children were playing and one grabbed onto the other. The parent went out to help and was grabbed by both children.

Station 2: One initial rescuer, one backup lifeguard, and two people needing rescue. Scenario: One conscious victim is violent and behaving erratically; the other follows directions.

Step 7—Reconvene to the deck to debrief the activity. Discuss the various methods the students used to meet the objectives of the rescue and the decision-making process that each rescuer went through in determining the course of action.

Instructor outcomes: Assessment of the students' skill level and problem-solving ability

Student outcome: Practical experience in making objective-based decisions

Closing Activity (5 minutes)

Step 1—Pass out closing statement cards to students (see appendix F for master for cards). Form a circle and ask each student to complete the sentence.

Instructor outcomes: Assessment of students' feelings about the training; identification of areas that need reinforcement

Student outcomes: Opportunity to give feedback on the training; transition to break

Facilitating Block 3

Goals	1. Introduce the concept of an emergency action plan (EAP).
	2. Review first aid for incidents common at aquatic facilities.
	3. Introduce land-based spinal-injury management.
	4. Introduce adjunct equipment.
	5. Conduct cardiopulmonary resuscitation (CPR) drills for adults, infants, and children.
Skill objectives	By the end of this block, students will be able to perform the following:
	1. Manual stabilization for suspected spinal injuries
	2. Standing takedown
	3. Adult CPR
	4. Child CPR
	5. Infant CPR
	6. Ventilation with a bag-valve mask (BVM)
	7. Use of a manual suction device
	8. Administration of emergency oxygen
	9. Use of an automated external defibrillator (AED)
Average time	4 hours (100 percent dry)
Overview	A. Preparing for block 3 (10 minutes)
	B. EAP builder—Who, What, When activity (25 minutes)
	C. Aquatic emergency care I (15 minutes)
	D. Aquatic emergency care II (45 minutes) S/L
	E. Land-based spinal-injury management (40 minutes)
	F. Introduction to adjunct equipment (40 minutes)
	Lisa G. CPR drills (60 minutes) L/S
	H. Closing activity (5 minutes)
Text reference	*StarGuard: Best Practices for Lifeguards, Third Edition*, chapters 2 and 8; *Essentials in Basic Emergency Care*, sections on first aid, CPR, AED, and emergency oxygen

(continued)

(continued)

Materials (See administrative guidelines in chapter 5 for per-student ratios.)	First-aid supplies or responder packs or both EAP cards Copies of blank first aid report from the StarGuard student text Pencils or pens Emergency care station cards Barrier masks Latex or vinyl gloves Backboards Bodily-fluids cleanup supplies Bag-valve masks Manual suction device Emergency oxygen Automated external defibrillator (AED) trainer Manikins and disinfectant supplies

Preparing for Block 3 (10 minutes)

Step 1—Greet students and read aloud the learner skill objectives for the block.

Emergency Action Plan Builder— Who, What, When Activity (25 minutes)

Step 1—Use the template in appendix C to print out EAP cards, or write out the EAP steps specific to your facility on index cards, one step per card. Mix up the cards and put them in a pile on the floor. Have each student pick out several cards, and ask the group to arrange the cards they have in their hands in the order in which the events would happen.

Step 2—Say, "Each card represents a step of *what* has to happen when managing an emergency. Now we are going to put together all of the individual cards that each of you have in your hand in an order to show *when* these steps should happen. In this emergency, someone is unconscious in the pool. I want you to put the card listing the first step here (indicate spot). Then arrange all the other steps in a long line going this way (indicate direction). If you have cards that list steps that might occur at the same time, it does not matter what order they are in—just as long as the general sequence makes sense." Allow your students about five minutes to arrange the sequence.

Step 3—Ask a student to loudly read the sequence that has been created. Say, "This determines the *what* and *when;* now let's determine the *who.* For this emergency action plan, or EAP, one lifeguard is the initial rescuer, one lifeguard serves as backup, and one manager is on site. Keep the cards in the same order, but now arrange them into three columns. This column (indicate spot) is for the initial rescuer. This column (indicate spot) is for the backup guard. This column (indicate spot) is for the manager." Allow about five minutes for the students to arrange the assignments.

Step 4—Say, "You've now created an emergency action plan for an unconscious person at a facility with two lifeguards and a manager. Look at the arrangement of the cards; this is called a flowchart, and you might see EAPs written and posted this way at the facility where you will work. For the next exercise, you work at a one-guard facility. You are the only person there, and your field supervisor is 45 minutes away. You know that all of these *what* steps must occur. What will you do? Arrange the cards into your EAP." Allow your students about five minutes to discuss and arrange the EAP cards. *Answer: Bystanders will have to be used, and some of the manager's tasks will be delayed.*

Step 5—Debrief the activity. Discuss how to get bystanders to help and how to deal with problems that can occur if bystanders try to interfere. Point out the following details:

- Be direct.
- Give clear step-by-step instructions.
- Stay calm.
- Don't let bystanders take over.
- Get the name, phone number, and address of bystanders.

Instructor outcome: Assessment of students' understanding of an EAP

Student outcomes: Practical understanding of the components of an EAP and active involvement in creating one for a specific situation; opportunity for critical thinking, teamwork, and group problem solving

Aquatic Emergency Care I (15 minutes)

Step 1—You can find the emergency care cards for this activity in the password-protected instructor area of the Starfish Aquatics Institute's intranet site at www.starfishaquatics.webexone.com. Introduce your students to the activity. Say, "You will be divided into groups of four, and each of you will perform one of the following roles: the injured or ill person, the responder who will manage the emergency, the manager who will complete the first aid report, and the evaluator. At each station will be a set of cards. The card for the ill or injured person will describe the scenario and list symptoms to exhibit. The responder card will list reminders on how to care for the injury or illness. The evaluator will watch the scenario and answer *yes* or *no* to the performance questions asked on the card. Each station will also include a blank first aid report form and a pen or pencil. The manager will complete the first aid report as part of the scenario. Bodily-fluids cleanup supplies will be available in case they are needed." Ask for four volunteers to demonstrate this activity for the rest of the class.

Step 2—Conduct the activity using the cards for a scrape. Debrief the activity by discussing questions from students. Use the evaluation card to provide guidance for the recommended treatment that should occur. If the question does not come up, ask, "Was it necessary to fill out a first aid report for a scrape?" *Answer: It depends on the policy and procedure of the facility where you work. Some facilities have a "band-aid log" for minor scrapes, others require a full report for every patron contact.* Rotate the four students into different roles.

Step 3—Conduct the activity using the cards for a nosebleed. Debrief the activity. Use the evaluation card to provide guidance for the recommended treatment that should occur. Rotate the four students into different roles.

Step 4—Conduct the activity using the cards for a laceration. Debrief the activity. Use the evaluation card to provide guidance for the recommended treatment that should occur.

Aquatic Emergency Care II (45 minutes)

Step 1—Before this activity begins, set up stations around the classroom, each with a set of cards for the scenario, blank first aid reports and a pen or pencil, bodily-fluids cleanup supplies, and props specific to the illness or injury. Decide if each group will receive a responder pack containing first aid supplies to be carried from station to station (preferred because it is more realistic and students will experience working from a hip pack) or if first aid supplies will be located at each station.

Step 2—Divide the class into groups of four and assign each to a starting scenario station. Allow five minutes per station, then rotate. Move among the groups and observe. Be available to clarify areas of concern and to keep students focused on the activity.

Instructor outcomes: Assessment of students' first aid knowledge, ability to take charge of a simulated emergency, and ability to complete a report

Student outcomes: Practical hands-on experience in approaching an injured or ill person, completing a report, and evaluating care provided by others; experience providing or observing care for the most common illnesses or injuries in an aquatic environment

Land-Based Spinal-Injury Management (40 minutes)

Step 1—Discuss mechanisms of injury in an aquatic environment. Ask, "What types of situations could cause spinal injury in an aquatic environment?" *Answers: Spinal injuries could be caused by diving into shallow water, being jumped on, hitting the edge of a diving board or slide, slipping and falling, hitting the edge of the pool, and so on.* Point out that a person with a suspected spinal injury in an aquatic environment is more likely to be standing up than floating in the water and is more likely to be conscious than unconscious.

Step 2—Demonstrate the standing takedown. Debrief the demonstration and emphasize these performance tips:

- Stand slightly off center from the victim in case he or she vomits.
- Talk to the person and inform him or her of what will happen before each step.
- Use your hands and arms to stabilize the person's spine, rather than immobilization devices. Avoid using immobilization devices unless you must extricate a person from the water.
- If a person with a suspected spinal injury is unresponsive, use the jaw-thrust maneuver to open the airway. If an effective airway cannot be obtained using the jaw-thrust, use the head-tilt, chin-lift, since airway is a priority.

Step 3—Divide students into groups of four to practice the standing takedown. Students should rotate through the roles of injured person, first rescuer, and backup rescuer after each performance. Have a backboard available for each group.

Instructor outcome: Evaluation of students' ability to manage a person with a suspected spinal injury in a standing position on land

Student outcome: Opportunity to practice the standing takedown

Introduction to Adjunct Equipment (40 minutes)

Step 1—Introduce emergency oxygen (approximately 10 minutes).

- Explain the following about emergency oxygen: Oxygen is essential for life. All unresponsive people with life-threatening illness or injury will benefit from emergency oxygen. In an emergency situation, oxygen can only help. If you are in doubt about the severity of the illness or injury, give oxygen. Do not delay basic emergency care for an ill or injured person in order to obtain or apply emergency oxygen if it is not immediately available.

- Identify and demonstrate the parts of an emergency oxygen system and their function:
  - Cylinder. This holds the oxygen; different sizes hold different amounts. Because the contents are under pressure, handle them carefully. The cylinder should be secured with a strap in a bag or case at all times.
  - Gauge. This indicates how much oxygen is in the cylinder. It should be checked and logged daily.
  - Pressure regulator and flow controllers. Settings may be preset or variable. Many emergency oxygen regulators are preset to deliver 6 liters per minute, but 15 liters per minute are necessary when connected to a bag-valve mask (BVM).
  - Tubing. Ensure that tubing is not kinked and that it is attached to the outlet on the regulator and the inlet on the mask or BVM.
  - Barrier mask with an oxygen inlet. This inlet allows oxygen to flow into the barrier mask. When you use the mask to provide ventilations during rescue breathing or cardiopulmonary resuscitation (CPR), the enhanced oxygen concentration will be provided to the nonbreathing person.

The oxygen flow rate should be set at the highest rate available. When emergency oxygen arrives at the scene where you are performing rescue breathing and CPR, switch masks or apply tubing to the mask already in use.

- Explain the following assembly procedures for an emergency oxygen system: Emergency oxygen systems at an aquatic facility should remain assembled during storage. You must practice with site-specific equipment to determine assembly needs.
- Demonstrate how to operate an emergency oxygen system:
  - Connect the tubing to the mask or BVM inlet if it is not already connected.
  - Turn on the oxygen flow.

- Verbally confirm to the rescuer that oxygen is flowing when you feel or hear it.
- For a conscious person, place the mask in close proximity to the person's airway or ask him or her to hold the mask. Describe to the person that oxygen is being used and that it is colorless, odorless, tasteless, and will help to support breathing. Tell the ill or injured person to breathe normally.
- For an unconscious person, place the emergency oxygen cylinder in a secured bag or case near the rescuer providing airway management, in a position that will not interfere with care. Confirm that the oxygen is flowing and hand the connected mask or BVM to the rescuer.
- Follow written directions and procedures from the manufacturer for compliance with federal regulatory requirements for labeling, refilling, storage, and safe handling.

Step 2—Introduce the bag-valve mask (approximately 5 minutes).

- Explain the purpose of a bag-valve mask: It provides ventilations without mouth-to-mask or mouth-to-mouth contact with an unconscious nonbreathing person. It provides a higher concentration of oxygen than the air you exhale into a victim during rescue breathing or the air from a bag-valve mask.
- Identify and demonstrate the parts and function of a bag-valve mask:
  - Mask
  - Bag
  - Oxygen reservoir
  - Tubing to attach to oxygen
- Identify the assembly procedure for a bag-valve mask: A bag-valve mask should remain assembled during storage. You must practice with site-specific equipment to determine assembly needs.
- Demonstrate how to use a bag-valve mask:
  - Use of a BVM requires at least two rescuers: one to maintain the victim's airway and seal the mask, the other to squeeze the bag and deliver ventilations.
  - Squeeze the bag.

Step 3—Introduce the manual suction device (approximately 5 minutes).

- Explain that the device removes liquid and small solid material from the victim's mouth and airway.
- Identify the parts of the device:
  - Tip
  - Reservoir
  - Handle
- Demonstrate how to use a manual suction device:
  - Slide the tip into the victim's mouth along the bottom cheek, not down the throat.

- Squeeze the handle fully. Repeat as needed.
- After the emergency, disinfect the device according to bodily-substance cleanup procedures.

Step 4—Introduce an automated external defibrillator (AED) (approximately 20 minutes).

- Explain that the purpose of an AED is to provide electrical shock to restart a heart that is in ventricular fibrillation.
- Identify and demonstrate the parts of an AED and their function:
  - Pads
  - On button
  - Shock button
- Identify the assembly procedure for an AED:
  - An AED is preassembled; however, some manufacturers require that the cord connecting the pads be plugged in. The AED prompt will direct this step.
  - You must practice with site-specific equipment to determine assembly needs.
- Demonstrate how to use an AED:
  - Move the victim several feet from the water's edge upon extrication to minimize the amount of water surrounding the victim.
  - If you are using emergency oxygen, turn off the oxygen and move the oxygen system away from the scene while using the AED. Return the oxygen if the AED prompts you to continue CPR.
  - It may be necessary to cut clothes, shave hair, or dry the area in order to apply the pads properly. Keep a razor and scissors with the AED response bag.
  - Turn on power to the AED. Listen to the prompts and follow directions from the AED.
  - In an aquatic environment it may be difficult to hear the AED prompts. Provide one rescuer to listen to the prompts and repeat them loudly.
  - Follow each advised shock with five cycles (about 2 minutes) of CPR, beginning with chest compressions.
  - For children ages 1-8, use child pads if available. If child pads are not available, use adult pads.
  - For all submersion incidents, and for all incidents involving unconscious children, provide five cycles (or about 2 minutes) of CPR before using AED. In cases where an adult has experienced a sudden collapse, provide immediate defibrillation.

Instructor outcome: Assessment of students' ability to use adjunct equipment

Student outcomes: Introduction to the purpose and use of emergency oxygen, a bag-valve mask, a manual suction device, and an automated external defibrillator

CPR Drills (60 minutes)

Step 1—Remind students that the body cannot survive when the heart stops and that external compressions can be used to circulate blood any time the heart is not beating. The combination of artificial ventilation (rescue breathing) and external chest compressions is called cardiopulmonary resuscitation (CPR).

Step 2—Demonstrate the hand and arm position and the rate, or count, for compressions for an adult, child, and infant. Debrief the demonstration and provide these performance tips, emphasizing delivery of effective chest compressions:

- Push hard and push fast. The chest should be compressed at a rate of about 100 compressions per minute for a person of any age.
- Rescuers should allow the chest to relax and return to normal position after each compression and use about equal compression and relaxation times.
- Children under one year of age are considered infants. Use the child guidelines for children about one year of age to the onset of puberty, which can be defined by observing secondary sex characteristics (breast development in girls or armpit hair in boys).
- The objective of CPR is to limit interruptions in chest compressions in order to keep the blood flowing. A single rescuer should use a ratio of 30 compressions to 2 breaths for a person of any age. Two rescuers should use a ratio of 30 compressions to 2 breaths for an adult, and a ratio of 15 compressions to 2 breaths when performing CPR on a child or infant.
- The rescuer's shoulders should be directly over the rescuer's interlocked hands for an adult or child. A rescuer may choose to use a single hand for a child. Location should be on the sternum between the nipple line.
- Rescue breaths should be delivered over 1 second and produce visible chest rise.
- For an infant, two rescuers should use the two-thumb, encircling hands technique (described in the *Essentials in Basic Emergency Care* text), which should include a thoracic squeeze. The thumb location should be just below the nipple line.
- The rescuer's knees should be against the person's body (for an adult or child) to allow for the best compression position. The person's arm should be lifted to allow the rescuer to position himself or herself against the body. Place infants on a hard surface.

Step 3—Set up a drill for practicing compressions using manikins. If manikins are not available, rescue tubes can be used for compression practice. Simulate the location of the sternum on the rescue tube and have rescuers demonstrate the correct hand placement and delivery of effective chest compressions.

Step 4—Divide students into groups of two or three, with an adult or child manikin and an infant manikin or practice doll. Students should have personal protective equipment. Set up practice drills for adult CPR, child CPR, and infant CPR, starting the sequence from assess, alert, attend.

Step 5—Divide students into groups of three. Two will be rescuers and one an unconscious person who is not breathing and has no pulse. Direct students to practice two-rescuer CPR (from assess, alert, attend) and integrate available adjunct equipment into the rescue scenario.

Instructor outcome: Assessment of students' adult, child, and infant CPR performance

Student outcomes: Hands-on experience performing compressions and alternating compressions with ventilations for an adult, infant, and child; hands-on experience using emergency oxygen, a bag-valve mask, a manual suction device, and an AED trainer

Closing Activity (5 minutes)

Step 1—Position students in a tight circle.

Step 2—Conduct the I Now Know That . . . activity.

Facilitating Block 4

Goals	1. Teach in-water spinal-injury management.
	2. Practice unconscious-victim rescues.
	3. Practice unconscious-victim protocol (UVP).
Skill objectives	By the end of this block, students will be able to perform the following:
	1. Ease-in entry
	2. Vise grip
	3. Vise-grip rollover and change-up
	4. Alternative vise grip
	5. Spinal rollover
	6. Ease-up to vise grip
	7. Two-person backboarding (shallow and deep water)
	8. Team backboarding (shallow and deep water)
	9. Standing takedown (in shallow water)
	10. Rescue breathing in the water
	11. Backboard pullout
	12. Unconscious-victim protocol (UVP)
Average time	4 hours (100 percent wet)
Overview Starraus	A. Preparing for block 4 (5 minutes)
	B. In-water spinal-injury management (90 minutes) *S/L*
	C. Unconscious-victim rescue and rescue breathing in water (25 minutes)
	D. Unconscious-victim extrication (15 minutes)
	E. Unconscious-victim protocol (75 minutes)
	F. Victim-recognition and aquatic-rescue scenarios (25 minutes)
	G. Closing activity (5 minutes)
Text reference	*StarGuard: Best Practices for Lifeguards, Third Edition,* chapters 10 and 11; *Essentials in Basic Emergency Care,* section on CPR
Materials *(See administrative guidelines in chapter 5 for per-student ratios.)*	Barrier masks
	Latex or vinyl gloves
	Rescue tubes
	Bodily-fluids cleanup supplies
	Backboards
	Emergency oxygen
	Bag-valve masks
	Manual suction device
	Automated external defibrillator (AED) trainer

Preparing for Block 4 (5 minutes)

Step 1—Greet students and read aloud the learner skill objectives for the block.

In-Water Spinal-Injury Management (90 minutes)

Step 1—Discuss the importance of recognizing the possibility of spinal injury based on the *presence* of a mechanism of injury, such as seeing a person dive into shallow water, strike a diving board, strike another patron, and so on (approximately 5 minutes).

Discuss the site-specific considerations for backboarding. Explain that conditions may differ from facility to facility and will influence the spinal-injury protocol in place. Variations may include the following:

- Directive of local emergency medical system (EMS). The 2005 First Aid Guidelines recommend that first aid providers use manual stabilization, rather than immobilization devices, to manage a suspected spinal injury until EMS arrives. However, for spinal injuries in the water, some EMS providers may want lifeguards to backboard and extricate the injured person from the water.

- Type of backboard available. Backboard features, such as wood or plastic construction, with runners or without, number and type of body straps, size, determine a facility's backboarding procedures.

- Physical conditions of the facility. Facility features, such as type of gutter system, whether the extrication area includes stairs or a beach entry, the presence of currents, and whether the space is confined, determine a facility's backboarding procedures.

- Number of lifeguards present and whether bystanders can be used. The backboarding protocol will be different for a one-guard facility than for a multiguard facility.

- In situations where less than three rescuers (including bystanders) are present, and a person with a suspected spinal injury must be extricated from the water, a head-immobilizer device will have to be used.

Emphasize that although the specific protocol and technique may vary from facility to facility, the *primary objective* for managing someone with a suspected spinal injury remains the same: minimize movement until EMS arrives. Explain that because the first step in minimizing movement of a person with a suspected spinal injury is to keep water movement to a minimum, an alternative form of entry into the water is necessary.

Step 2—Demonstrate an ease-in entry (approximately 5 minutes). Debrief the demonstration and point out these performance tips:

- Use this entry if another type of entry would create waves that could move the injured person. This usually occurs if the person is within 20 feet of your entry point.

- It is not necessary to use this entry if a compact jump will not move the water around the injured person. This is usually the case if the person is more than 20 feet from your entry point.

Step 3—Demonstrate on land and in the water the technique for rescuing a person with a spinal injury who is floating faceup (vise grip) and floating facedown (vise-grip rollover and change-up) (approximately 10 minutes). Debrief the demonstration and emphasize these performance tips:

- Time is crucial if a victim is facedown because the person cannot breathe.
- Signal for backup *before* making contact with the person.
- Grasp the person's arms between the elbow and shoulder and do not adjust the position after contact has been made.
- Use of a rescue tube is optional in shallow water but necessary in water deeper than chest level.
- If you will perform backboarding, the vise-grip rollover requires a change-up to move the rescuer's arm from under the injured person. Wait as long as possible to make the change-up in order to provide maximum support.

Step 4—Divide students into pairs and conduct a practice drill for the vise grip and vise-grip rollover and change-up skills in both shallow water and deep water with a rescue tube (approximately 15 minutes).

Step 5—Demonstrate on land and in the water the alternative vise grip and the spinal rollover (approximately 10 minutes). Debrief the demonstration and emphasize these performance tips:

- Use the alternate vise grip to eliminate the need for a change-up when a backboard is immediately available and maximum support is not needed.
- Use the spinal rollover technique when an injured person does not have enough shoulder flexibility to squeeze his or her head with the arms.
- During a spinal rollover, the rescuer's top arm should be positioned along the victim's sternum and the bottom arm along the spine so that the arms are parallel.

Step 6—Divide students into pairs and conduct a practice drill for the alternative vise grip and the spinal rollover (approximately 10 minutes).

Step 7—Demonstrate backboarding in shallow water using two-person backboarding, team backboarding, and a standing takedown (approximately 20 minutes). When conducting the three backboarding demonstrations, rotate students through the rescuer roles. Debrief the demonstration and emphasize these performance tips:

- The objective is to minimize movement of the head, neck, and spine until EMS arrives.
- Strap the chest, then the rest of body.
- When at least three rescuers are present, one rescuer should manually maintain spine stabilization during extrication, and after extrication until EMS arrives. If enough rescuers are not present to manually maintain spine stabilization during extrication, and the person must be removed from the water, apply a head immobilization device (HID) to maintain spine stabilization during extrication.
- Check the straps before extrication.

- Try to backboard and extricate the victim in less than two minutes to reduce the person's chance of developing hypothermia.
- After extrication, maintain manual spine stabilization, monitor the victim's airway, breathing, and circulation (ABCs), keep the victim warm, and provide emergency oxygen if available. If the person becomes unresponsive, use a jaw-thrust maneuver to open the airway. If an effective airway cannot be established using this maneuver, open the airway with the head-tilt, chin-lift method.

Step 8—Demonstrate backboarding in deep water using either a two-person backboarding technique or team backboarding (approximately 10 minutes). Debrief the demonstration and emphasize these performance tips:

- The objective is to minimize the movement of the head, neck, and spine until EMS arrives.
- The first choice is always to move to shallow water if possible.
- Apply a HID only when manual spine stabilization cannot be maintained during extrication.
- You may place rescue tubes under the backboard to provide additional stability in deep water.

Explain that, although it is unlikely, a person with a suspected spinal injury may be submerged and not floating on the surface. Emphasize again the importance of observing a mechanism of injury before suspecting a spinal injury. Say, "When you assess a situation that involves a submerged person, you should suspect a spinal injury only if you saw something happen that would lead you to believe that a spinal injury occurred. Otherwise, you should consider this person a drowning victim and immediately provide airway management because time is crucial."

Step 9—Demonstrate the ease-up to vise grip (approximately 5 minutes). Debrief the demonstration and point out these performance tips:

- Make just enough contact with the injured person to initiate a weightless rise to the surface.
- The rescue tube should be in position so that as soon as the person is within reach and near the surface, you can initiate a vise grip using a smooth transition.
- This transition eliminates the bouncing and bobbing at the surface that is common with other techniques, and one rescuer can perform it.

Instructor outcome: Evaluation of the students' ability to meet objectives of spinal-injury management in the water

Student outcome: Hands-on practice of spinal-injury management skills

Unconscious-Victim Rescue and Rescue Breathing in the Water (25 minutes)

Step 1—Demonstrate how the rear and leg-wrap rescues can be used to manage an unconscious victim in the water. Debrief the demonstration and emphasize these performance tips:

- The techniques are the same as those used for a conscious victim.
- Place the rescue tube lower than the victim's shoulder blades so that the victim's arms can be pulled back around the tube and so that the head will drop back into an open airway position.
- Move away from the victim to a position behind the head.
- The facility EAP should include a procedure for transporting a mask to the water in the event of an unconscious-victim rescue (e.g., attached to the rescue tube or carried in a hip pack).

Step 2—Organize your students in a semicircle, standing in shallow water. If you are outdoors, place yourself so that the students are not looking into the sun.

Step 3—Demonstrate how an unconscious victim lying on a rescue tube naturally assumes an open-airway position.

Step 4—To demonstrate how the mask makes a seal in the water, have each student place a mask over his or her mouth and nose and lean back into a submerged position with the valve above water to maintain breathing ability.

Step 5—Demonstrate a rescue (starting from the STAAR rescue components) of an unconscious drowning victim and begin rescue breathing in the water. Debrief the demonstration and emphasize these points:

- Rescue breathing in the water is necessary if you will not be able to move the victim from the water to the deck within about 30 seconds.
- Rescue breathing in the water takes place while you and the victim move toward the takeout point. It does not delay care, but rather begins the basic life support sequence sooner.
- Do not check for a pulse while in the water. It takes up time, and it is difficult to feel a pulse while in the water. Other signs of circulation indicate cardiac involvement. For example, a person has a pulse if he or she is moving, coughing, or breathing. If these signs are absent, assume that the person has no pulse.

Step 6—Divide the class into pairs or small groups and conduct a practice drill for rescue breathing in the water. Have the students perform rescue breathing at the adult rate (10 to 12 breaths per minute, approximately one breath every 5 to 6 seconds), followed by the child and infant rate (12 to 20 breaths per minute, approximately one breath every 3 to 5 seconds). Remind students to ask another student's permission before placing a barrier mask on his or her face during practice.

Unconscious-Victim Extrication (15 minutes)

Step 1—Demonstrate the backboard pullout, using a backboard without straps to extricate an unconscious person who is not suspected of having a spinal injury. Debrief the demonstration and emphasize these points:

- This technique reduces the risk of injury to the rescuer and victim.
- Backboards are required equipment at pools and therefore are readily available.
- This technique allows a large person to be removed effectively by a smaller rescuer. Small victims can be lifted out without using a backboard.

Step 2—Divide students into groups to practice the backboard pullout.

Unconscious-Victim Protocol (75 minutes)

Step 1—Demonstrate the following steps of the unconscious-victim protocol:

- STAAR
- Rescue breathing in the water
- Backboard pullout
- Basic life support on the deck consisting of CPR with oxygen and an AED

Debrief the demonstration and emphasize these points:

- Dipping latex gloves in the water makes it easier and faster to put them on with wet hands.
- Backup rescuers should attempt to put on gloves while going to the scene. CPR should not be significantly delayed to put on gloves.
- Extricate the victim to a position at least six feet (1.8 meters) from the water's edge, if possible.
- During CPR, the rescuer performing compressions should raise the victim's arm so that the rescuer can position his or her knees against the victim's body.
- Visually locate the correct compression position on the sternum between the nipple line. The rescuer's shoulders should be aligned over the hands during compression.
- It is likely that the victim will vomit before or during CPR. If vomiting occurs, roll the victim away from rescuers to avoid contact with the vomit and bodily fluids. A suction device can help remove vomit from the victim's mouth and airway.

Step 2—Divide students into groups of four or five, with one victim and one initial rescuer. The other rescuers will bring the equipment, help with extrication, turn on oxygen, assist with victim care as needed, turn on the AED, and call out prompts.

Step 3—Provide time for each student group to practice the UVP for an adult, child, and infant.

Victim-Recognition and Aquatic-Rescue Scenarios (25 minutes)

Step 1—Divide students into groups and have them rotate between stations every five minutes. If possible, position students in lifeguard stands and have them blow their whistles during the simulated rescues. Explain to students that this activity serves as a review and practice for the skills test. Set up the following drill stations, and move students through full rescues as quickly as possible:

Station 1—Unconscious-victim protocol for a child

Station 2—Unconscious-victim protocol for an adult, supplemented with adjunct equipment, such as emergency oxygen, AED, suction, and BVM

Station 3—Unconscious-victim protocol for an infant

Station 4—Conscious drowning victim on the surface

Station 5—Conscious drowning victim submerged

Station 6—Two-guard rescue for conscious drowning victim

Instructor outcome: Evaluation of students' ability to manage aquatic rescues

Student outcomes: Opportunity to practice and build confidence

Closing Activity (5 minutes)

Step 1—Position students in a tight circle.

Step 2—Conduct the I Now Know That . . . activity.

Facilitating Block 5

Goals	1. Define and reinforce StarGuard best practices behaviors. 2. Evaluate cognitive knowledge. 3. Evaluate performance capability. 4. Complete course paperwork. 5. Identify professionalism, personal safety, and liability considerations.
Skill objectives	The purpose of this block is attitude development and review and assessment of knowledge and skill rather than skill development.
Average time	4 hours (50 percent wet, 50 percent dry)
Overview	A. Preparing for block 5 (5 minutes) B. Written exam (40 minutes) *Lisa* C. Good, bad, ugly (15 minutes) *Stair* D. Bad things happen to good people (30 minutes) E. What to expect from your employer (20 minutes) F. Evaluation scenarios (90 minutes) G. Course completion authorization (30 minutes) H. Closing activity (10 minutes)
Text reference	*StarGuard: Best Practices for Lifeguards, Third Edition*, chapter 12 and chapter 13 and all chapters for review. *Essentials in Basic Emergency Care*, all chapters.
Materials *(See administrative guidelines in chapter 5 for per-student ratios.)*	Barrier masks Latex or vinyl gloves Rescue tubes Bodily-fluids cleanup supplies Backboards Emergency oxygen. Manual suction device Bag-valve masks Automated external defibrillator (AED) trainer Paper and pens or pencils Written exam Answer sheets Answer key Authorization forms Props for Good, Bad, Ugly activity

Preparing for Block 5 (5 minutes)

Step 1—Greet students and read aloud the learner skill objectives for the block.

Written Exam (40 minutes)

Step 1—Distribute the written exam and answer sheet. Instruct students to put all answers on the answer sheet—they should not write on the test. The exam is closed book. In special circumstances, you may deliver the exam orally for students who have difficulty taking written exams.

Step 2—Use the answer key to grade the exam. Provide students a copy of their graded answer sheet and a test so that they can view the questions missed and identify the correct answers.

Instructor outcome: Verification of cognitive knowledge

Student outcomes: Reinforcement of cognitive knowledge

Good, Bad, Ugly (15 minutes)

Step 1—Select three people to assist with this activity. Provide one person with all of the props necessary to portray a *good* lifeguard: rescue tube, sunglasses, hat or visor, lifeguard shirt, lifeguard shorts, nametag, whistle, hip pack, sunscreen, and water. Provide the second person with a rescue tube, one identifying piece of apparel, and a whistle to portray a bad lifeguard. Provide the third person with a rescue tube, whistle, cell phone, and a magazine or book to portray the ugly lifeguard.

Step 2—Explain to your actors that the *good* lifeguard should exhibit only exceptional behaviors such as visible scanning, excellent posture, staying hydrated, changing posture often, courteous patron relations, and so on. The *bad* lifeguard does not do anything obvious, but should exhibit marginal behavior such as whistle twirling, slouching, fidgeting, looking bored, yawning, nail biting, skin picking, grooming, and inconsistent scanning. The *ugly* lifeguard should exhibit irresponsible behavior such as talking on the cell phone, reading, sleeping, trying to distract the *bad* guard with social conversation, walking away from the zone, talking about other staff members, and so on.

Step 3—Set up three chairs in the front of the room. Ask your students to make three columns on a blank sheet of paper and title them Good, Bad, and Ugly.

Instruct the class to watch the three lifeguards on duty and write down the behaviors they notice in each category.

Step 4—Bring in the actors and let them role-play for about five minutes.

Step 5—Debrief the activity. Ask, "What made the lifeguard good? What made the lifeguard bad? What made the lifeguard ugly?" After each question, elicit responses from your students about what they observed. Use what occurred during the role-playing to lead into discussions about leadership, role modeling, and group dynamics. For example, ask, "What happened to the bad guard's behavior when the ugly guard was around?" *Answer: Weak people usually are pulled down to the lowest behavior modeled rather than up to a higher standard and that's what happened to the bad guard.* Encourage additional discussion by asking questions such as the following: Which of these lifeguards would you want as your backup in an emergency? What would you do if you had to work with an *ugly* lifeguard? Have you ever been in a similar situation? How did you handle it?

Instructor outcome: Evaluation of students' ability to understand StarGuard best practices behavior.

Student outcomes: Ability to think critically and compare behaviors and the consequences of the behaviors; reinforcement of expected StarGuard best practices behavior

Bad Things Happen to Good People (30 minutes)

Step 1—Lead a discussion about the moral, ethical, and legal responsibilities of being a lifeguard. Questions you might use to start or redirect the discussion include the following:

- "Should a lifeguard accept an after-hours private-party job where equipment is unavailable and he or she is not expected to enforce rules?" *Answer: No, not unless the person hiring the lifeguard provides in writing full release of the lifeguard from liability and this release is reviewed by the lifeguard's attorney.*
- "Should an off-duty lifeguard stop to rescue someone in an open-water setting without equipment?" *Answer: In this case, a lifeguard is acting as a Good Samaritan, because he or she is not on the job and required to respond. Rescuing someone in this instance poses an extremely high risk and presents a personal choice that the student should consider carefully.*
- "Should lifeguards answer questions from the media, attorneys, or others?" *Answer: No. They should direct requests for comment or information about a rescue or incident to a supervisor or designated spokesperson.*
- "What is the best way to protect against liability?" *Answer: Performing at the highest level possible in the five areas of the Starfish risk management model and maintaining skills at rescue-ready levels through in-service training are the best ways to prevent liability.*

Step 2—Discuss examples of situations that have resulted in litigation. Share stories of real-life incidents if possible.

What to Expect From Your Employer (20 minutes)

Step 1—If all of your students will be your employees, use this time to provide site-specific information.

Step 2—If any of your students will not be your employees, use this time to reinforce and answer questions about what he or she should expect from an employer. Say, "As we've just discussed, many circumstances may occur while you are lifeguarding that could influence the rest of your life. It will be your responsibility to make sure that your employer provides you the necessary equipment, supplemental training, and support to do your job in a way that minimizes the risk of these things happening. What should you expect your employer to provide?" *Answers include the following:*

- Personal protection equipment, such as gloves and barrier mask
- Rescue tube
- Umbrella or shade
- Water to drink
- Lifeguard identification such as a uniform item
- Communication or signal device
- Telephone with EMS (9-1-1) access
- First aid supplies
- A break from scanning at least every hour
- Ability to change position to stay alert and to see the bottom while scanning
- Orientation to and practice of the facility's emergency action plan
- Training in handling hazardous materials and in chemical safety, if pool maintenance is required
- Orientation to and practice with the rescue equipment, such as backboard, AED, and oxygen
- Orientation to facility operating procedures
- Ongoing enrichment training
- Ongoing performance assessment
- Coverage under a liability insurance policy or immunity from liability

Step 3—Lead a discussion based on areas of concern or items that need clarification.

Evaluation Scenarios (90 minutes)

Step 1—Evaluate single-rescuer adult, child, and infant CPR skills. If you have a second instructor, set up stations and rotate your students through these stations as they wait to perform a team-management scenario.

Step 2—Evaluate team management of aquatic emergencies. Develop several scenarios that integrate all rescue skills as realistically as possible. Give each student a chance to play the lifeguard in a scenario, and have the student start in a guard stand, from which he or she will enter the water. Begin each scenario by blowing a whistle or horn. The students playing backup guards should respond when they hear the signal, coming from a location where they would usually be, such as the break room. They should bring equipment to the scene from where it would usually be located in your facility, and they should put on gloves if the scenario would cause them to come into contact with the victim. All students should participate in the rescue from start to finish.

All students should participate in at least one scenario involving all of the following skills:

- Scanning and proactive rotation

- Conscious-person rescue
- Unconscious drowning victim management (including post-rescue cleanup of bodily substances)
- Suspected spinal-injury management

Step 3—Debrief after each scenario. Discuss what went well, what didn't, and why. Using the following criteria, determine if the performance met the objectives of the rescue:

- The students' actions would not have contributed to the injury or death of the victim or the rescuer.
- The students' declining to take action would not have contributed to the injury or death of the victim or the rescuer.

Step 4—The instructor may assign to students who do not meet the rescue outcomes during the first trial an additional test scenario. If the student does not meet reasonable performance standards during the second trial, the instructor may require the student to complete instructor-prescribed remediation before being evaluated again. The instructor may also require the student to take the StarGuard course again.

Course Completion Authorization (30 minutes)

Step 1—Fill in and sign the instructor portion of the Course Completion Authorization forms, including all sections of the student card with the exception of the student's name.

Refer to the *Training Center Administrative Guide* for questions about completing the form.

Step 2—Distribute the Course Completion Authorization forms to your students.

Step 3—Instruct the students to fill out the top section through the e-mail address and then stop. Remind students to press hard so that all three copies are legible.

Step 4—When students have completed the top section, guide them through the following information:

- Training center that conducted your training (Fill in the official training center name.)
- Location where you took your training (Fill in the name of the pool used.)
- New student or renewal (new = new to StarGuard; renewal = renewal of StarGuard)
- Course completion date (Fill in current date.)
- Location where you will be working (Provide if known.)

Step 5—Say, "I want you to read the next section very carefully. It is the Statement of Understanding. Before you sign it, I want to make sure that you don't have any questions about what it means. One of the statements is that you agree to follow the StarGuard Best Practices. Turn your form over. Listed on the back are the behaviors you agree to maintain. Are there questions about best practices?" Discuss as needed.

"Now read the Statement of Understanding, and if you have questions, raise your hand and I'll be right over to help clarify what it means. If you agree to abide, sign and fill in the date on the line by the statement."

Step 6—Say, "Next, write your name on the line indicated in the card section at the bottom right of the form. Now, on the line labeled Authorization Number, I want you to make sure that the preprinted number on the top of the form matches the number in that space. Since the wallet card section of the form can be detached, transferring the preprinted number allows the national office to track your paperwork by using the authorization number on your wallet card.

Step 7—Say, "Next, I want you to complete the course evaluation. I hope this course has been as rewarding an experience for you as it has been for me. Please be honest in your evaluation because this is what will help us provide the best training possible. If you would like to make additional comments, please use the back of the top (white) copy."

Closing Activity (10 minutes)

Step 1—Issue Course Completion cards and Authorization forms

Step 2—Thank your students for their time and wish them well.

Appendix A

Block Plan Summary Chart

							Summary of integrated components				
Recommended time to complete: 4 hours per block	Average time in minutes	Presentation	Learning experience	Student will develop knowledge of these concepts:	Student will develop these motor skills and practical applications:	Equipment	VRT	Bloodborne	CPR	First aid	AED/O2
Block 1 **Outcomes:** 1. Gauge student experience level and swimming ability 2. Begin team building 3. Introduce basic life support (BLS) and bloodborne pathogens skills in order to provide a foundation for students to be able to perform integrated CPR scenarios later in the course 4. Begin to develop in students a change in attitude regarding the importance of and risks related to the job of a lifeguard 50 percent wet 50 percent dry	15	Activity	Setting the climate Have You Ever . . . ? Name Toss Challenge			Soft tossable item Have You Ever . . . ? question cards Hat or basket for holding cards					
	50	Activity	Water skills screening and course orientation		Approach stroke with a rescue tube Feetfirst surface dive and retrieval of an object from the bottom	Rescue tubes Diving brick or submersible manikin Beach balls or similar type of balls					
	30	Discussion and demonstration	Bloodborne pathogens and bodily-substance isolation using pretest, recreational water illness (RWI) discussion, and cleanup demonstration	Importance of scene safety and isolating bodily substances Concept of universal precautions Techniques for controlling exposure to and cleanup of bodily fluids Importance of patron education in preventing RWIs	Use of personal protective equipment Putting latex or vinyl gloves onto wet hands Bodily-substance cleanup Proper removal of latex or vinyl gloves	Bloodborne pathogens pretest Pens or pencils		✓			
	30	Activity	Bloodborne pathogens and bodily-substance isolation using Blood, Feces, Vomit activity			Latex or vinyl gloves Bodily-fluids cleanup kit		✓			
	Break										
	15	Drill	Chain of survival	Chain-of-survival concept and components of the Starfish Survival Model	Emergency response sequence Initial assessment of an unconscious person, including 9-1-1 call	Latex or vinyl gloves Barrier masks Manikins Who Wants to Be a Lifeguard? questions Study guides		✓	✓		
	40	Drill	Airway management	Airway management, breathing management, and circulation assessment according to American Heart Association (AHA) CPR and emergency cardiac care (ECC) guidelines	Head-tilt, chin-lift method Placement of barrier mask Pulse check and assessment of signs of circulation Foreign body airway obstruction (FBAO)			✓	✓		
	30	Activity	Airway management: emergency care sequence and rescue breathing Rewind activity suggested		Emergency response and basic life support (BLS) rescue breathing sequence for adult, child, infant			✓	✓		
	20	Discussion	Who Wants to Be a Lifeguard?	Important role of the lifeguard							
	10	Review	Closing activity: I Now Know That . . .								

(continued)

							Summary of integrated components				
Recommended time to complete: 4 hours per block	Average time in minutes	Presentation	Learning experience	Student will develop knowledge of these concepts:	Student will develop these motor skills and practical applications:	Equipment	VRT	Bloodborne	CPR	First aid	AED/O2
Block 2 **Outcomes** 1. Define risk management and prevention strategies 2. Begin victim recognition training (VRT) 3. Provide practical scanning and surveillance experience 4. Develop skills for conscious-victim rescue 75 percent wet 25 percent dry	10	Discussion	Setting the climate								
	15	Activity	Starfish risk management model	Importance of early intervention		Pens or pencils and paper					
	30	Activity	Prevention assessment Walk-about	Risk factors in an aquatic environment and the layers-of-protection model		Pens or pencils and paper					
	20	Activity	Victim-recognition training (VRT) Where's Timmy?	Concept that water hides and suffocates	Identification of simulated victim on the bottom	Submersible manikins Shadow dolls Symptom cards	✓				
	45	Activity	Victim-recognition training (VRT) Starfish scanning system Assignment of numbers for scanning practical experience and evaluation	Factors that determine zone size Priority of constant, dedicated surveillance Reasons for a scanning system: RID factors (why) 3-D triage scanning (where) 10-second scan (when) 5-Minute Scanning strategy (how)	Scanning patterns and 3-D triage scanning 10-second scan and 5-Minute Scanning Strategy Proactive rotation	Rescue tubes	✓				
	25	Discussion	Victim-recognition training (VRT) Victim school	Behavior characteristics of distress and drowning	Victim simulation		✓				
	Break										
	30	Drill	Aquatic rescue: STAAR, compact jump, escape	Functions of 3 observation skills (scan, target, assess) and two response skills (alert and rescue)	Whistle blast Compact jump Emergency escape	Rescue tubes Whistles	✓				
	30	Drill	Aquatic rescue: front, rear, two guard	Advantages of using a rescue tube Importance of talking to a person being rescued Criteria for successful rescue	Front rescue Rear rescue Two-guard rescue		✓				
	30	Drill and scenario	Aquatic rescue: leg wrap, multiple victim	Importance of knowing the objectives of a rescue to assist in decision making	Leg-wrap rescue: standard and extended Multiple-victim rescue		✓				
	5	Review	Closing activity: I Now Know That . . .			Closing statement cards					

Recommended time to complete: 4 hours per block	Average time in minutes	Presentation	Learning experience	Student will develop knowledge of these concepts:	Student will develop these motor skills and practical applications:	Equipment	VRT	Bloodborne	CPR	First aid	AED/O2
Block 3 **Outcomes:** 1. Introduce the concept of an emergency action plan (EAP) 2. Review first aid for incidents common at aquatic facilities 3. Introduce land-based spinal-injury management 4. Introduce adjunct equipment 5. Conduct CPR drills for adults, infants, and children All dry	10	Discussion	Setting the climate					✓		✓	
	25	Activity	EAP builder Who, What, When activity	Components of an EAP and the roles of various people who respond to emergencies		EAP cards		✓		✓	
	15	Demonstration	Aquatic emergency care I	Symptoms and common causes of illness or injury in an aquatic environment		First aid supplies or responder packs Emergency care station cards Bodily-fluids cleanup supplies		✓		✓	
	45	Scenario	Aquatic emergency care II		First aid treatment of injury and illness Completion of a first aid report			✓		✓	
	40	Discussion Drill Scenario	Land-based spinal-injury management	Conditions and symptoms that raise suspicion of head, neck, or spinal injuries	Manual stabilization for suspected spinal injuries Standing takedown	Backboards Latex or vinyl gloves				✓	
	40	Discussion Activity	Introduction to adjunct equipment	Usefulness of and safety precautions for adjunct equipment	Administration of emergency oxygen Ventilation with a bag-valve mask (BVM) Use of a manual suction device Use of an AED	Bag-valve masks Emergency oxygen Manual suction device AED trainer	✓	✓			✓
	60	Drill	CPR drills	Recommended compression position, hand placement, body position, rates, and ratios to perform effective CPR	Adult CPR Child CPR Infant CPR Integration of adjunct equipment	Barrier masks Manikins and disinfectant supplies Emergency oxygen Bag-valve masks Manual suction device AED trainer Latex or vinyl gloves Emergency oxygen		✓	✓		✓
	5	Review	Closing activity: I Now Know That . . .								

(continued)

Recommended time to complete: 4 hours per block	Average time in minutes	Presentation	Learning experience	Student will develop knowledge of these concepts:	Student will develop these motor skills and practical applications:	Equipment	VRT	Bloodborne	CPR	First aid	AED/O2
Block 4 / Outcomes: / 1. Teach in-water spinal-injury management / 2. Practice unconscious-victim rescues / 3. Practice unconscious-victim protocol (UVP) / All wet	5	Discussion	Setting the climate							✓	
	90	Discussion drill (from STAAR)	In-water spinal-injury management	Techniques for providing manual stabilization for a person with a suspected in-water spinal injury / Importance of knowing the local EMS provider protocol / Importance of obtaining site-specific training	Ease-in entry / Vise grip / Vise-grip rollover and change-up / Alternative vise grip / Spinal rollover / Ease-up to vise grip / Two-person backboarding (shallow and deep water) / Team backboarding (shallow and deep water) / Standing takedown (in shallow water)	Rescue tubes / Backboard with head immobilization device (HID) / Towel / Emergency oxygen	✓			✓	
Break											
	25 / 15	Drill (from STAAR)	Unconscious-victim rescue and rescue breathing in the water / Unconscious-victim extrication	Method for rescue breathing in the water and using a backboard to extricate an unconscious person from the water	Unconscious-victim rescue / Rescue breathing in the water / Backboard pullout	Rescue tubes / Barrier masks / Backboard (no HID)	✓		✓		
	75	Scenario (from STAAR)	Unconscious-victim protocol (UVP)	Considerations for basic life support of drowning victims / Considerations for integrating adjunct equipment into a rescue in progress / Technique of putting a wet hand into a wet latex or vinyl glove to minimize the time it takes to put on the gloves	Unconscious-victim protocol (UVP)	Rescue tubes / Barrier masks / Backboards (no HID) / Latex or vinyl gloves / Cleanup supplies for bodily fluids / Emergency oxygen / Bag-valve mask / Manual suction device / AED trainer	✓	✓	✓		✓
Break											
	25	Scenarios	Victim-recognition and aquatic-rescue scenarios			All as stated previously	✓		✓		✓
	5	Review	Closing activity: I Now Know That . . .								

							Summary of integrated components				
Recommended time to complete: 4 hours per block	Average time in minutes	Presentation	Learning experience	Student will develop knowledge of these concepts:	Student will develop these motor skills and practical applications:	Equipment	VRT	Bloodborne	CPR	First aid	AED/O2
Block 5 **Outcomes:** 1. Define and reinforce StarGuard best practices behaviors 2. Evaluate cognitive knowledge 3. Evaluate performance capability 4. Complete course paperwork 5. Identify professionalism, personal safety, and liability considerations 50 percent dry 50 percent wet	5	Discussion	Setting the climate								
	40	Activity	Written exam			Written exam Answer sheets Answer key	✓	✓	✓	✓	✓
	15	Activity	Good, Bad, Ugly	Factors that create or take away from a professional image		Uniforms Rescue tubes Other props					
	30	Discussion	Bad things happen to good people	General principles of legal liability and negligence related to lifeguarding							
	20	Discussion	What to expect from your employer	Equipment, training, and support that your employer should provide							
	90	Activity	Evaluation scenarios			Rescue tubes Latex or vinyl gloves Backboards Emergency oxygen Manual suction device Bag-valve mask AED trainer Cleanup supplies for bodily fluids	✓	✓	✓	✓	✓
	30	Activity	Course completion authorization	StarGuard Statement of Understanding		Authorization forms					
	10	Activity	Closing activity: award of course completion cards								

Appendix B

Sample Outline for Parent Orientation Meeting

(Suggested time: 40 minutes)

I. Welcome and introduction
II. Purpose of meeting
    A. To inform the parents of lifeguard candidates under the age of 18 of what lifeguarding today involves, including the risks, rewards, and expectations
    B. To provide details about the course and logistics
II. StarGuard course
    A. Prerequisites
    B. Logistics—course dates, times, expectations (be on time, be ready to work, and so on)
    C. StarGuard Authorization and Agreement form
III. StarGuard best practices and expectations
    A. Hiring process
    B. StarGuard best practices (sunscreen use, uniforms, professionalism, and so on)
    C. StarReview performance accountability audit
    D. What an employer will expect of the lifeguard
    E. What the lifeguard should expect of an employer
IV. Summary—the "why" of risk management
    A. Reduce liability risk for facility and lifeguard
    B. Protect the lifeguard from health risks
    C. Provide a professional working environment
    D. Provide the best patron environment with the best chance to save lives
V. Questions and other information

Appendix C

Emergency Action Plan Cards Master

Scan
Target
Assess
Alert
Rescue

Cover
rescuer's zone
OR
clear the pool.

Bring
backboard and
emergency
care equipment
to takeout
point.

Call 9-1-1.

Remove victim from water (extricate).

Glove up.

Open airway.

Look, listen, feel (for normal and adequate breathing).

(continued)

Provide basic life support according to CPR guidelines.

Incorporate oxygen and AED (if available).

Transfer care to EMS.

Assist at scene as needed.

Identify victim and locate family or friends on site.

Gather victim's belongings.

Meet EMS and direct them to the scene.

Obtain witness statements.

(continued)

(continued)

Clean up site and equipment of biohazards.

Prepare rescue report.

Recover equipment taken from the scene by EMS.

Control crowd and onlookers.

Notify
supervisor,
administration,
and owners.

Conduct a
postincident
debriefing.

Arrange
for critical
incident–stress
debriefing.

Contact
Starfish
Aquatics
Institute.

(continued)

(continued)

Prepare media statement according to facility policy.

Manage communication with media according to facility protocol.

Participate in critical incident–stress debriefing or counseling.

Create cards for facility-specific components.

Appendix D

Have You Ever . . . ?
Questions Master

Have you ever saved someone's life?

Have you ever made a rescue?

Have you ever worked as a lifeguard?

Have you ever performed CPR on a real person?

111

(continued)

Have you ever cleaned up blood?

Have you ever cleaned up vomit?

Have you ever cleaned up feces from a pool?

Have you ever seen examples of bad lifeguarding?

Have you ever taken a CPR class?

Have you ever taught a life-guard class?

Have you ever taken a lifeguard class?

Have you ever been a role model for children or your peers?

113

(continued)

Have you ever been responsible for saving a human life?

Have you ever been to a waterpark?

Have you ever gone scuba diving?

Have you ever gone surfing?

Have you ever gone kayaking?

Have you ever been seriously injured?

Have you ever swum a mile?

Have you ever been on a blind date?

(continued)

Have you ever driven a boat?

Have you ever lost your car keys?

Have you ever been a patient in a hospital?

Have you ever been to Europe?

Appendix E

Who Wants to Be a Lifeguard? Questions Master

1. Describe the worst lifeguarding you've ever seen. Why do you consider it the worst?

2. Describe the best lifeguarding you've ever seen. Why do you consider it the best?

3. What motivated you to become a lifeguard?

4. Have we done things in class so far that you never expected to have to do while lifeguarding?

5. What do you think most people's image of a lifeguard is? What should it be?

6. What do you think will be your biggest challenge?

Appendix F

Closing Statement Cards Master

I learned

_____

I feel

_____

I'm wondering

_____

_____

I've rediscovered

_____

_____

119

(continued)

I'm more confident about

_____

_____

I've figured out

_____

_____

I appreciated

_____

_____

I felt challenged by

_____

_____

Appendix G

Block Plan Summary Chart for Blended or Challenge Course

Recommended time to complete: 8 hours	Average time in minutes	Presentation	Learning experience	Student should already have knowledge of these concepts:	Student will develop these motor skills and practical applications:	Equipment	Summary of integrated components				
							VRT	Bloodborne	CPR	First aid	AED/O2
Outcomes: 1. Gauge students' experience level and swimming ability 2. Evaluate students' cognitive knowledge 3. Provide students with practical scanning and surveillance experience 4. Practice and evaluate students' aquatic rescue skills 5. Practice and evaluate students' emergency care and CPR skills 6. Evaluate students' performance capability 7. Issue course completion cards	40	Activity	Written exam			Written exam Answer sheets Answer key	✓	✓	✓	✓	✓
	10	Activity	Setting the learning climate Have You Ever . . .? Name Toss Challenge			Soft tossable item Have You Ever . . .? question cards Hat or basket for holding cards					
	30	Activity	Water skills screening		Approach stroke with a rescue tube Feetfirst surface dive and retrieval of an object from the bottom	Rescue tubes Diving brick or submersible manikin Beach balls or similar type of balls					
	15	Activity	Victim-recognition training (VRT) Where's Timmy?	Concept that water hides and suffocates	Identification of simulated victim on the bottom	Submersible manikins Shadow dolls Other props	✓				
	5	Activity	Communication signals	Need for communication signals	Blowing a whistle	Whistles	✓				
	10	Demonstration and activity Each student rotates in for at least one 10-min. shift throughout the course	Victim-recognition training (VRT) Starfish scanning system Assignment of numbers for scanning practical experience and evaluation	Factors that determine zone size Priority of constant, dedicated surveillance Reasons for a scanning system: RID factors (why) 3-D triage scanning (where) 10-second scan (when) 5-Minute Scanning Strategy (how)	Scanning patterns and 3-D triage scanning 10-second scan 5-Minute Scanning Strategy Proactive rotation	Rescue tubes Whistle	✓				
	10	Demonstration and drill	Aquatic rescue: STAAR, compact jump, escape	Functions of three observation skills (scan, target, assess) and two response skills (alert and rescue)	Whistle blast Compact jump Emergency escape						
	45	Demonstration and drill	Aquatic rescue: front, rear, two guard, leg wrap, multiple victim	Advantages of using a rescue tube Importance of talking to a person being rescued Criteria for a successful rescue	Front rescue Rear rescue Two-guard rescue Leg-wrap rescue: standard and extended Multiple-victim rescue						
	15	Scenarios	Aquatic rescue: conscious-person scenarios (in water)	Knowing the objectives of a rescue to assist in decision making			✓				
	15	Demonstration and scenarios	Land-based spinal-injury management	Conditions and symptoms that raise suspicion of head, neck, or spinal injuries	Manual stabilization for suspected spinal injuries Standing takedown	Backboards Latex or vinyl gloves Emergency oxygen		✓		✓	✓

(continued)

(continued)

Recommended time to complete: 8 hours	Average time in minutes	Presentation	Learning experience	Student should already have knowledge of these concepts:	Student will develop these motor skills and practical applications:	Equipment	Summary of integrated components				
							VRT	Bloodborne	CPR	First aid	AED/O2
	45	Demonstration	Aquatic emergency care I	Importance of scene safety and isolating bodily substances; Concept of universal precautions; Techniques for controlling exposure to and cleanup of bodily fluids; Importance of patron education in preventing RWIs		First aid supplies or responder packs; Emergency care station cards; Cleanup kit for bodily fluids		✓		✓	
		Scenarios and evaluation activity	Emergency care II: conscious-person scenarios (land based)	Symptoms and common causes of illness or injury in an aquatic environment	First aid treatment of injury and illness; Bodily-substance cleanup; Proper removal of latex or vinyl gloves; Completion of a first aid report	First aid supplies or responder packs; Emergency care station cards; Cleanup kit for bodily fluids; Emergency oxygen		✓		✓	✓
Break											
	10	Demonstration	Chain of survival	Chain-of-survival concept and components of the Starfish Survival Model	Emergency response sequence; Initial assessment of an unconscious person including 9-1-1 call	Latex or vinyl gloves, Barrier masks, Manikins	✓	✓	✓	✓	✓
	35	Demonstration and drill	CPR review for adults, infants, and children; Single rescuer; Two rescuer; Integration of adjunct equipment	Airway management, breathing management, and circulation assessment according to American Heart Association (AHA) CPR and emergency cardiac care (ECC) guidelines	Head-tilt, chin-lift method; Placement of barrier mask; Pulse check and assessment of signs of circulation; Rescue breathing sequence for adults, infants, and children; Foreign body airway obstruction (FBAO); Adult CPR, Child CPR, Infant CPR; Administration of emergency oxygen; Ventilation with a bag-valve mask (BVM); Use of a manual suction device; Use of an AED	Barrier masks; Manikins and disinfectant supplies; Emergency oxygen; Bag-valve masks; Manual suction device; AED trainer; Latex or vinyl gloves; Emergency oxygen		✓	✓		✓
	20 / 15	Drill	Unconscious-victim management: rescue breathing in the water; Unconscious-victim extrication	Method for rescue breathing in the water and using a backboard to extricate an unconscious person from the water	Unconscious-victim rescue; Rescue breathing in the water; Backboard pullout	Rescue tubes; Barrier masks; Backboard (no HID)	✓	✓	✓		✓
	45	Demonstration and scenarios	Aquatic rescue: unconscious-victim protocol	Basic life-support considerations for drowning victims; Considerations for integrating adjunct equipment into a rescue in progress; Technique of putting a wet hand into a wet latex or vinyl glove to minimize the time it takes to put on the gloves	Unconscious-victim rescue; Rescue breathing in the water; Backboard pullout		✓	✓	✓		✓
	30	Demonstration and scenario	Aquatic rescue: in-water spinal-injury management	Techniques for providing manual stabilization for a person with a suspected in-water spinal injury; Importance of knowing the local EMS provider protocol; Importance of obtaining site-specific training	Ease-in entry; Vise grip; Vise-grip rollover and change-up; Alternative vise grip; Spinal rollover; Ease-up to vise grip; Two-person backboarding (shallow and deep water); Team backboarding (shallow and deep water); Standing takedown (in shallow water)	Rescue tubes; Backboard with head-immobilization device (HID); Towel; Emergency oxygen	✓			✓	✓

Recommended time to complete: 8 hours	Average time in minutes	Presentation	Learning experience	Student should already have knowledge of these concepts:	Student will develop these motor skills and practical applications:	Equipment	Summary of integrated components				
							VRT	Bloodborne	CPR	First aid	AED/O2
	45	Scenarios	Evaluation scenarios			Rescue tubes Latex or vinyl gloves Backboards Emergency oxygen Manual suction device AED trainer Cleanup supplies for bodily fluids	✓	✓	✓	✓	✓
	30	Discussion	Authorization of course completion	Statement of Understanding		Authorization forms					
	10	Activity	Closure activity: award of course completion cards			Authorization forms					

Bibliography

Allen, I. Elaine, and Seaman, Jeff. 2004. *Entering the mainstream: The quality and extent of online education in the United States, 2003 and 2004.* Massachusetts: Sloan Consortium.

American Heart Association. 2003. International Liaison Committee on Resuscitation (ILCOR) advisory statement: Recommended guidelines for uniform reporting of data from drowning. *Circulation.*108:2565. Retrieved January 16, 2005 from the American Heart Association Journal's Web site: http://circ.ahajournals.org/cgi/content/full/108/20/2565.

Branche, C.M. and S. Stewart (Eds). 2001. *Lifeguard effectiveness, a report of the working group.* Retrieved April 10, 2004 from the Center for Disease Control and Prevention, National Center for Injury Prevention and Control Web site: www.cdc.gov/ncipc/lifeguard/LifeguardReport.pdf.

Center for Development and Population Activities. 1995. *Training trainers for development.* Washington DC: Author. Retrieved May 8, 2005 from the CEDPA Web site: www.cedpa.org/publications/pdf/trainingtrainers_english_all.pdf.

Covey, S. 1998. The empowered learning model. Retrieved January 1, 2005 from the Franklin Covey Web site: www.franklincovey.com/forbusiness/facilitator/elm/print/index.html.

Covey, S. 2004. *The 8th habit: From effectiveness to greatness.* New York: Free Press.

About the Author

Jill E. White founded the Starfish Aquatics Institute in 2000 with the mission to reduce drowning and save lives by providing reputable, responsive aquatic safety training programs to the public. In 2005 she was named one of the Top 25 Most Influential People in Aquatics by *Aquatics International magazine*, and she has appeared on the US Water Fitness Association's Who's Who in Aquatics: Top 100 Professionals list for the past four years.

In the past, White has authored textbooks on lifeguarding, lifeguarding instruction, and swim instruction for the National Safety Council, Jeff Ellis & Associates, and the American Safety & Health Institute. She has firsthand experience in training, supervising, and managing lifeguards and has taught thousands of lifeguards and hundreds of lifeguarding instructors. She has presented educational sessions at conferences for the National Recreation and Park Association; World Waterpark Association; American Alliance for Health, Physical Education, Recreation and Dance; Athletic Business Conference; and numerous state and regional events.

White enjoys reading, hiking, and aquatic sports. She lives in Savannah, Georgia, with her husband, Robbin.

HUMAN KINETICS
The Information Leader in Physical Activity

Starfish Aquatics Institute and Human Kinetics team up to provide outstanding aquatics education and safety courses and resources.

The Rising "STAR" in Aquatic Education

THE BEST LIFEGUARD TRAINING

Protect your patrons and your lifeguards by providing an integrated curriculum of emergency care skills that exceed national standards but with cost and service advantages that keep training time to a minimum!

THE BEST SWIM INSTRUCTION

Teach people to swim for pleasure, fitness, or competition, but teach them correctly through Starfish Swim School! We offer a complete swimming instruction system for all ages and abilities.

RUN A SAFE AND EFFICIENT OPPERATION

The StarReview(tm) program follows the Starfish Risk Management Model, evaluating performance in prevention, surveillance, aquatic rescue, emergency care, and professionalism/personal safety.

RAISE WATER SAFETY AWARENESS

Safety Training and Aquatic Rescue (STAR)® is an awareness level water safety program designed for non-lifeguards such as parents and caregivers, pool and slide attendants, water exercise instructors, health club and resort personnel, and swimming coaches.

PARTNER WITH THE BEST IN THE BUSINESS

The Starfish Aquatics Institute offers a new approach to providing aquatic training and risk management services to aquatic facilities with an all-inclusive program that designates your aquatic facility or agency as a Training Center. There are five levels of Partner Plans to choose from!

Through the new Starfish Aquatic Education Center, Human Kinetics will develop and deliver online courses and associated resources to expand Starfish Aquatics Institute's existing curriculums with courses including:
- StarGuard lifeguard and Starfish Swim School Instructor courses
- Safety Training and Aquatic Rescue (STAR) courses
- Pool Chemistry & Pool Operator course
- Pool Manager course

2/06

For more information about Starfish programs please call the national office at 912-692-1173 or visit our web site at www.starfishaquatics.org